SOLDAT XI C

World War II German Reenactor Guide and Combat Uniform & Equipment Reproductions

By Cyrus A. Lee

Pictorial Histories Publishing Co., Inc.
Missoula, MT

LIBRARY OF CONGRESS
CONTROL NUMBER 2001 135882

ISBN 1-57510-088-6
First Printing 2001

Typography and layout by Jan Taylor
on Macintosh utilizing: Aldus PageMaker 6.5, Adobe Photoshop 5.0

Cover graphics by Egeler Design
Cover Photography by Cyrus Lee

Companion Volumes:
Vol. I – Equipping the German Army Foot Soldier in Europe in 1939 – 1942
Vol. II – Equipping the German Army Foot soldier in Europe in 1943
Vol. III – Equipping the German Army Foot Soldier in Europe 1944 – 1945
Vol. V – Uniforms and Insignia of Panzerkorps Großdeutschland 1939 – 1945
Vol. VI – Equipping the Waffen ϟϟ Panzer Divisions 1942 – 1945
Vol. VIII – Fallschirmjäger
Vol. XI – The Reproductions – The Post War Years

Future Companion Volumes:
Vol. VI – Equipping the German Army Foot Soldier in Southern Europe and North Africa 1940 – 1945
Vol. VII – Equipping the Waffen ϟϟ Panzergrenadier Regiments 1942 – 1945
Vol. X – Corrections and Additions
Vol. XI B - The Reproductions – The Post War Years
Vol. XII – Norwegian Volunteers 1940 – 1945

Companion Series:
Canuck – The World War II Canadian Military Collector's Handbook
Tommy – The Collector's Historical Perspective to the British Soldier of The Second World War

Future Companion Series:
G.I. – The World War II American Military Collector's Handbooks
Ivan – The World War II Soviet Military Collector's Handbooks
Muskitier – The World War I German Army Collector's Handbooks
Poilu – The World War I French Military Collector's Handbooks
Doughboy – The World War I American Military Collector's Handbooks

SOLDAT XI C

World War II German Reenactor Guide and Combat Uniform & Equipment Reproductions

By Cyrus A. Lee

PICTORIAL HISTORIES PUBLISHING COMPANY, INC.
713 South Third West, Missoula, Montana 59801
(406) 549-8488 phpc@montana.com

Table of Contents

Table of Contents cont.

Acknowledgements

Without support and help from these folks this work would not have become what is has today. I know that I have missed some, and I apologize. Thanks to you all! Cyrus Lee

Marshall Weiss, Eric Toby, and Vincent Milano. Fred Poddig, Dale Taylor, Kent Peters, Robby Fraker, and Randy Arneson *1. ϟϟ L ϟϟ AH.* Bob Lawrence, *Großdeutschland.* Paul Meda, *3. Pz. Gren. Div. Div.* Drew Wilhelm Zigo. Don Calder, *2. Fallschirmjäger.* John Figueroa, *Panzer Lehr.* Jon Grossardt, Travis Jacobsen, *12. ϟϟ Hitlerjugend.* Joseph Starost, *3. /ϟϟ Aufklarung Abt.* Michele Milunas. Erin Warfield. Mike Bollow, *116. Pz. Div. 'Windhunde', & 2. Pz. Div.* Rocco Spencer, *1. Fallschirmjäger.* Tony Dudmann. Mike Dunn, *Feldgendarmerie Trupp 200. 21. Panzer.Div. 2. Fallschirmjäger.* Claudio Ortellie. Kevin Poole.

A note of special thanks to Ed and Maria Walton. Thanks for your witness in Christ Jesus during my stay in Dallas. Those days spoke volumes to my heart and made a difference in my life and that of FamLee.

Dedication

To William Cyrus Lee
"But Dad, they're
Krauts!"

Introduction

SOLDAT XI C is divided into sections dealing with uniforms, headgear, footwear, equipment, camouflage and protective garments; *Fallschirmjäger* specific articles, weapons, barracks impressions and personal items; heavy equipment; and Female Impressions. The *Zeitgeist* photos provide the example of "those moments" experienced by historical reenactors. "Honoring Those We Remember" shows what one unit is doing to promote the connection between veteran and reenactor. As always, *Der alte Hase* is present to provide information and insight into organizational and technical helps.

Waiting for the enemy.

The majority of photos by the Soldat FHQ Kriegsberichter Zug: Cyrus Lee, Rachel Putnam, & Robert Kelleher with all other contributions noted in acknowledgements section.

Preface

This is the second *SOLDAT* book loaded with historical replicas!

Participating in and supplying World War II German historical reenactors has led me on a new path that I find exciting and, as a collector, terrifying! In this book I wanted to accomplish two major goals. First, I have been asked repeatedly to produce a book that would provide a basic guide to historical reenactors. Second, I have been asked repeatedly to produce a follow on to *SOLDAT Volume XI The Reproductions—The Post War Years.* In *Volume XI C* I have done both.

World War II reenacting grows daily. Once centered in areas of high population, now individuals and small groups are spring up around the country to recreate history. As with American Civil War Reenacting, the demand for "authenticity" rises. In this book you will see the state of the art of reenacting as of April 2001. I have not covered every unit in existence, but the cross section will provide a good photo overview. Included are some basic information guides. Mostly supplied by *1. SS LSSAH,* one of the oldest and premiere German organizations, and by Marshall Weiss. These will help newly organizing groups form. As with American Civil War reenacting, suppliers rise up to meet the demand for uniforms and equipment; this, however, is an information and how to book, not a vendor sourcebook.

When I first put reenactor photos into a *SOLDAT* book, I received letters from collectors criticizing my choice. They felt that reenactors were not "keepers" of historical artifacts, but "destroyers," wearing uniforms and equipment to shreds in the field. While this was possibly a fact in the early years, I found very few truly guilty. What I did find were historians who collected original militaria to provide resources for producing newly made, historical replicas and who tried to insure that how they created their "first person impression" was totally correct—to the stitch. I found that for the collector, the danger was not the misuse of valuable collectibles; the danger was the same one that has plagued and continues to plague us—misrepresentation of replicas as originals.

Today as I write this, I can access via print or electronic medium numerous vendors selling combat uniforms, equipment, etc. I will make a flat, "educated" statement that no less than 50% of the items sold as originals on the collectible market today are copies. This percentage increases—with the level of collector desirability—to probably 90% plus in the case of *Waffen ᛋᛋ* items. Not all vendors are purposefully deceptive, but many are. As I have operated *SOLDAT FHQ*—my online source of German military replicas—the horror stories and tales of deceit have poured in. I am faced daily with the opportunity to sell my aged replicas as originals at an auction house for an astronomical profit. I have repeatedly requested one of the major auction houses to carry *Volume XI* as a customer resource, but they refuse. I know what is going on in the collecting market place, and a good portion is rotten!

Reenactors drive a very competitive business that produces uniforms and equipment. These replica pieces are daily becoming more and more like original uniforms and gear! What was the standard when I wrote *Volume XI* is now ridiculed as "farb" (the term used by the reenacting world to define something that is not historically correct.) The reenacting community is NOT guilty of producing fakes to be used to dupe collectors. They seek instead to fulfill the needs of their hobby and put their money into businesses that perform that function. Unfortunatly, many collectors have not read books like *Volume XI* and don't recognize even these older replicas as what they are—FAKES! These collectors have no chance with these newer, stitch–perfect copies. As a source of replica militaria, I am aware that some of the items I sell are being remarketed as originals. I have spotted them on sites and in catalogs and have taken appropriate action. However, neither I—nor any of the other firms producing items—can control what goes on with our product once it leaves our hands. We can take steps to identify items and publish information about them, but it is the consumer who must be aware and educated. Here, in the collecting side of this book, learn and be safe. Herein also lies a blessing for those who are willing to use replicas in their collections or those who are large–scale model builders, wishing to create full–scale displays—you need no longer pay outrageous prices for "originals;" there are top–notch substitutes available.

As with *Volume XI,* this book will cause collectors heartache as they spot their "100% original" item on these pages. The learning continues. Take this book and *Volume XI* with you to shows; you'll get far better results as the vendor will have to prove his wares are correct. *Volume XI B* is on the way for more fake identification! For my reenacting *Kamraden* present and future, I hope that this small effort is of help to you.

Enjoy *SOLDAT!*

Cyrus

Die Uniform
The Uniform

Bluse, Hosen, u. Mantel
Tunics, Trousers, & Overcoats

The M36 Uniform

The classic German military tunic and trouser combination. The *Feldbluse* or tunic has a five–button front with dark badgecloth collar and *Schulterklappen* or shoulder insignia for *Heer* applications. The tunic transitioned through varying shades of *feldgrau. Heer Litzen* or Army collar insignia may be either in branch *Waffenfabe* or general issue, normally sewn onto separate backing and then applied to the collar. All four pockets are of the scalloped style and are pleated. The tunic has four places where a series of three reinforced eyelets allow for the use of the *Seitenhaken* or belt hooks visible in the photo. These hooks attach to the ends of the *Tragegurte* or the internal cartridge belt support straps, which are fitted into the tunic lining. The tunic is worn closed at the throat, held in place by a small hook and eye fitting.

Field and garrison uniforms can make use of several basic uniform types or styles. While the German military did

The *Tuchhose* or long trousers worn in this photo are the standard—straight leg, button fly, and three internal pockets, held up by means of *Hosentrager* or suspenders. These trousers can be worn with *Schnüschuhe* or lace–up shoes, *Schnürstiefel* or lace–up boots, or with *Marchstiefel* or marching boots. These trousers are correct in variations of *steingrau* or *neugrau*, which is medium gray without any green hues as well as in shades of *feldgrau*.

not make use of system that designated uniform item styles by "M years," in most cases these are used, as they are an established reference point for reenactors and collectors alike. Two premises apply to the reenactor when choosing a uniform style. First, the reenactor should be aware and comply with his unit's regulations. Second, if there is no guidance from the unit, the *SOLDAT* rule of thumb is that you can reenact the entire war period in a early pattern uniform, but you can't reenact the entire war period in a late war uniform. *Waffen* ᛋᛋ units can follow these guidelines as well, substituting appropriate insignia. This applies for the *Heer* units as well, when photos show ᛋᛋ insignia on the uniform.

The M40 Uniform

Cut identically to the M36 this style lacks only the dark–green badgecloth collar and was produced in varying shades of *feldgrau. Heer Litzen* or Army collar insignia is normally the general issue sewn directly to the collar. *Schulterklappen* may vary from dark–green to *feldgrau* for *Heer* applications. The trouser normally issued with this uniform would be the same as with the M36 uniform.

German tunic evolution did not jump from the M40 directly to the classic M43 style. Photo evidence shows progressions of changes in pockets, button number, and other fine points. One replica firm offers this transition tunic as an M42. The classic M43 has non–pleated box pockets with squared flaps, six–button front and no provision for the internal *Tragegurte,* which were abolished from general issue in 1943. The *Seitenhaken* are held in place by four short, web straps sewn to the tunic walls. The tunic is produced in various shades of *feldgrau.* Collar *Litzen* is the general issue style sewn in place.

Der alte Hase

Tunic Pocket Contents

Tunic pockets were normally bulging when the Soldat was in the field. Contents were distributed by need and handedness. The upper pockets contained the Soldbucher, letters, photos and wallet, a notebook with pen or pencil. The lower pockets contained clean socks, toilet articles, fork/spoon combination, cigarettes, tobacco, and matches, perhaps a scarf or gloves. If room remained clean underwear finished the load.

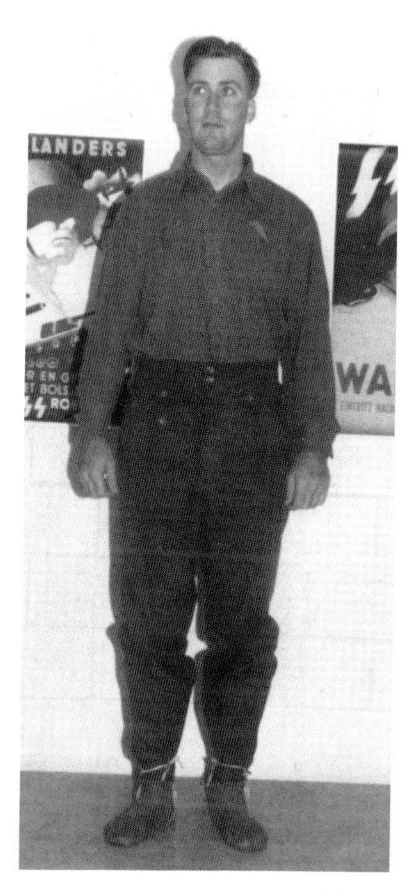

Acceptable trousers for use with this tunic would be the *Tuchhose* or the *Keilhose* shown. The *Keilhose* or mountain trousers were patterned after popular civilian ski trousers. These have a tapered leg for better fit with short boots and organic stirrup (as shown in the accompanying photo) that kept the leg in the boot or *Gamashen.* The *Keilhose* have a reinforced seat and button down belt loops. Waist size can be adjusted by mean of side buckles and straps.

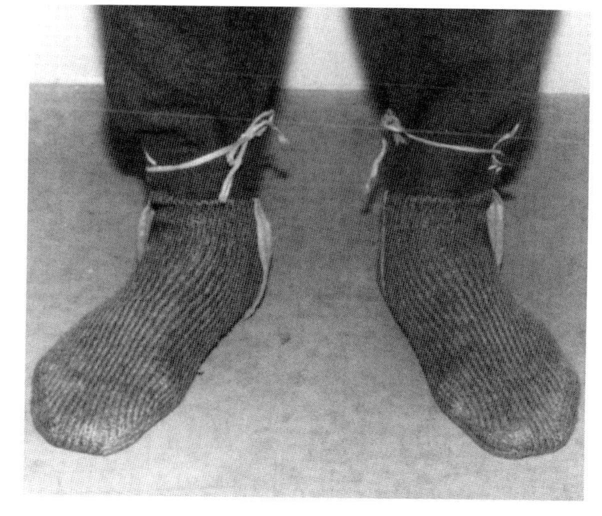

Keilhose have organic stirrups, which keep the cuff in the boot or *Gamaschen.*

The M44
Uniform

The *Waffen* ϟϟ produced their own variation of this tunic with five–button front closure with only two eyeholes for each *Seitenhaken.*

The *Felduniform 44* or M44 field uniform was the final progression in German combat uniforms of WWII. (cont. p 9)

The short *Feldbluse 44* is complemented by the *Feldhose 44* that may or may not have a cloth belt with three–prong buckle either inside the waistband or tacked to the outside of the waistband and running through the belt loops. The belt shown in this photo is not attached and is a separate item. Trouser details are clear in this picture. These were designed with a drawstring cuff made to snug around the ankle under the *Gamaschen.* A very practical uniform, contrary to much that is said about acceptance by the *Soldat,* it was obtained and used whenever possible. Unfortunately it is not applicable for anything but late war battles.

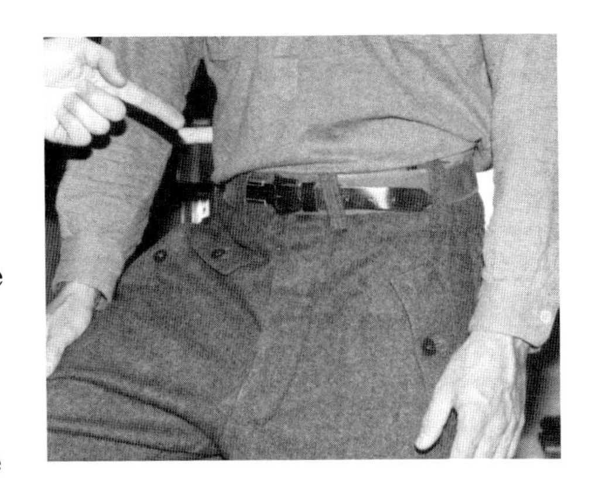

Photo evidence supports use of the *Feldbluse 44* by general grade officers in late '44 and '45. Officers made use of both issue and custom tunics.

Feldbluse für Offiziere or officer field blouse or tunic changed little in design through out the war. These are far more than a modified M36 tunic and are actually a completely tailored garment. As the war progressed the *feldgrau* cloth changed, so varied shades are very acceptable.

These *Waffen* ᛋᛋ officers show use of three distinct shades of *feldgrau* in their M36 tunics. The inspecting officer wears the *Stiefelhose* or breeches. The officer to his left wears *Tuchhose* or long trousers.

The uniform was to be produced in a *Feldgrau 44* wool, which had a distinct olive brown hue. However, any available wool was utilized and makes any *feldgrau* acceptable.

Distinct details of the *Waffen SS Feldgrau Feldbluse u. Hose für Panzertruppe*—in this case either armored artillery or assault artillery.

While normally worn open at the neck, the *Feldbluse* could be buttoned to the neck to provide a second layer of wool cloth for protection against the elements.

The *Heer* version of the *Feldbluse für Panzertruppe.*

A *Heer Panzersoldaten* with *Sd. Kdz. 231* armored car.

A *Heer Feldherrenhalle Panzeroffiziere* waits the order to move.

A two–pocket version of the *Hemd* or shirt. Various manufacturers are producing these as well as the collarless white shirt.

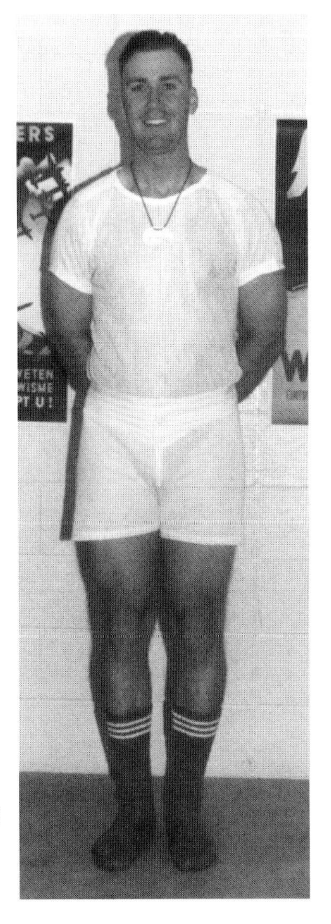

Extreme realism—beginning his impression by wearing original tropical underwear!

The *Sporthemd* worn as a warm weather work shirt by this *Grossßdeutschland Waffenmeister* while in the process of producing *Erkennungsmarken* for new soldiers.

Wearing the *Mantel* or overcoat, this *Heer Soldaten* presses forward. Shown is the second pattern of overcoat produced (distinguished by the small collar made of *feldgrau* cloth) used from 1940 onwards, fitting into any war period. Prior to 1940 the overcoat collar was covered in dark green badgecloth. This version fits into any war period impression.

Below, the rear view of the *Mantel* as worn by *Großdeutschland Küchenunteroffizier* as he labors at the *Feldküche* or field kitchen trailer. A *SOLDAT* note: *GD* has excellent period food in the field, a real time and space travel mechanism. It doesn't take a *Feldküche* to provide this touch of realism for any unit, but this is certainly an enhancement!

Der alte Hase

Feld Lebensmittel
Field Rations

Unlike the American Army, the *Landser* did not normally eat out of a boxed, pre–packed combat ration. The German soldier consumed *Proviant* or *Futter* of basic foods such as *Brot* or bread, *Käse* or cheese, *Fleisch* or meats, *Obst* or fruit, *Gemüse* or vegetables, etc., that was provided by his *Versorgungs–, Fleischerei–, and Bäckerei–Kompanie* or supply, butcher, and bakery companies.

Komißbrot or military bread was a staple for all meals and was baked in the field. It is a whole grain bread that was issued in loaves and then rationed by cutting the loaf. The *Soldat* was provided bread usually once a day in the field at *Mittagessen* or lunch. His ration was to last until the next lunch. It was at *Mittagessen* that the *Essenträger* or soldiers detailed to carry the hot meal of the day delivered the *Futter*. The *Kochgeschirr* or mess kit was filled at this time. Additional rations were also distributed for *Abendessen* or the evening meal and *Frühstück* or breakfast. Both of these meals culturally usually consisted of cold foods such as *Wurst* or sausage, *Schmalz* or other spreads, fresh or dried fruit, and bread with exception of a hot drink such as *Kaffee* or coffee. *Kaffee* was the standard beverage carried in the *Feldflasche* or canteen, as it covered the taste of the water when boiled. *Kaffee* was drunk hot (heated on the *Eisbitkocher*) or cold.

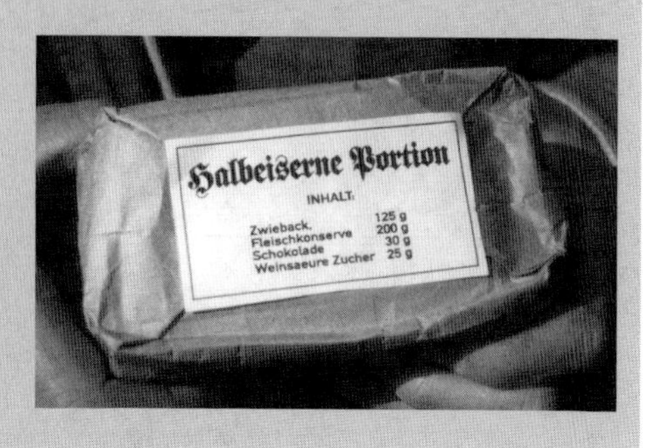

The uneaten portion of the day's ration was carried in the *Kochgeschirr* or in the *Brotbeutel* or bread bag. Fat content of the meals was as high as possible, so when the meals in the mess kit cooled they congealed. Bread could also be added to thicken the contents to increase transportability. Upright, "incorrectly mounted" mess kits in period photos may well depict a *Soldat* not wanting to loose any of his *Lebensmittel.* Spreads (see *der alte Hase* Recipe for *Schmalz*) were carried in the *Fettbüsche* or fat container.

The German reenactor can substitute many off–the–shelf items from the modern supermarket, and provide the necessary packaging. In the case of the rations above, this consists of putting the items in their proper carrier. If wrapped at all, food would be put in cellophane or brown paper—no tinfoil or plastic wrap. Some units provide hot meals, others not. Suitable soups and stews can be found in the market, cooked and put into the *Kochgeschirr* prior to taking the field. *Wurst* was produced in the field in large, not individual, portions. The *Wurst* was rationed by cutting. The same with *Käse.* A small unit may well be able to provide rations authentically to itself by going to the grocery store.

While there has been research into late–war German rations patterned after the American K–Ration, the *Nahkampfpäckchen* and the *Großkampfpäckchen*, like reproducing K–Rations this has proved difficult from standpoint of both production and legal sale. To overcome this, labels have been created to cover modern packaged food products (see photos.) While not 100% authentic, this certainly looks better than many other options. Providing labels and information as to what kinds of canned food are acceptable in the field the unit can insure all its members have a uniform and reasonably authentic ration. I find these to also be a great conversation starter in the waiting areas of the airport.

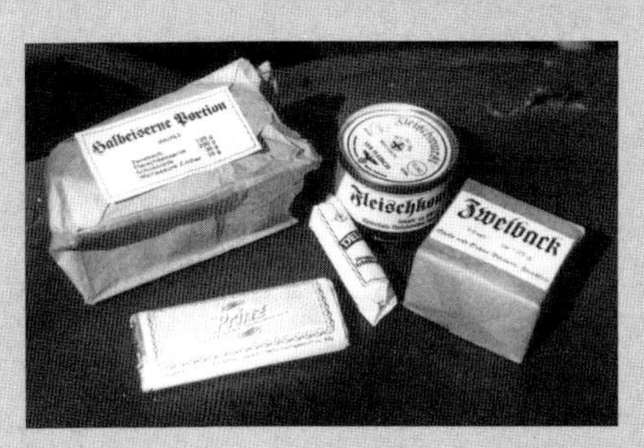

This *Waffen* ᛋᛋ *Grenadier* stands watch outside the barracks. He is wearing the *Mantel* without collar insignia.

This *Waffen* ᛋᛋ *Spieß* wears the third pattern *Mantel* or greatcoat with larger collar. Production of this coat began in 1942, so it fits into any mid– to late–war impression. The display of insignia is correct; numerous period photos show a mixture of overcoats with and without collar insignia.

The interior of the third pattern *Mantel* was made from rayon or artificial silk. The unit has placed period posters on the barracks's wall as well as made use correct bedding.

Two styles of *Ledermantel für Offizier* are shown here, one in *feldgrau* the other in *schwartzleder.* The *Handschuh* or gloves are *Bundeswehr* issue.

The *Drillichjacke* in its original form, a work jacket. Left the color of the flax fiber used to produce the hard–wearing *Drillich* fabric with its characteristic chevron or herringbone weave. This cloth had long been produced to make work clothing in the civilian population. These tunics were ordered dyed to a *feldgrau* color in 1938, then in 1940 the *schilfgrün* or reed green color was adopted.

Introduced in 1942 as a summer uniform, the new *Drillichjacke und Hosen* were cut identically to the service tunic and trousers. Tunics came with standard collar *Litzen* and National Eagle. Loops and buttons were provided for shoulder insignia. Buttons were mounted with split ring "S" clips, so they could be removed for laundering.

No *Drillich* cloth headgear was widely produced; standard practice was to wear wool issue caps or helmet. The happy *Großdeutschland Schütz* wears a civilian shirt under the tunic. The helmet is camouflaged with a piece of material from the *Zeltbahn* held in place by a length of inner tube rubber.

Großdeutschen mit Fahrrad wearing *Drillichanzug.* These have all changed colors from wash and wear.

A unique *Turkistan* volunteer impression at FIG 2001. Collectors, nothing is impossible to reproduce!

A *Kriegsmarine* rating at FIG 2001. Created from replica *Bundesmarine* and *Volksmarine* uniform items.

A *Kriegsmarine* coat, which began as military surplus. Much is available to those who seek and know how to assemble a uniform.

A *Kaptitanleutnant* in walking out uniform at FIG 2001. With the popularity of U–Boats at an all time high, it would be wise of collectors to beware of what they are purchasing.

A *Leutnant* of *21.Pzr Div. in Nord Afrika.* Tropical uniforms are being produced by at least three separate firms at this time. With increased interest in this aspect reenacting, this may well grow. The tropical officer belt and buckle are reproduced as well, having been available on the market longer than the uniforms.

An enlisted *Feldgendarm* tropical uniform.

This group shot, taken during a California–based DAK event in April 2001, shows the range of tropical uniforms available. This includes the boots—tall as shown, as well as the ankle style—manufactured by a US firm.

Der alte Hase

Bekleidung und Ausrüstung
Wear of Uniform and Equipment
by Erich Toby and Marsh Wise

One of the first events that started the transition from German civilian to *Landser,* was the issue of common military uniforms and equipment. The following regulations govern the actual wearing or carrying of some of the more common items of uniform and equipment used by the German soldier. For a correct impression, the proper wearing (and upkeep) of these items is as important as the authenticity of the items themselves. Learn the German names!

HEADGEAR

M-43 *Einheitsfeldmütze:* one finger above the right ear, and two fingers above the left ear. The side flaps are not to be unbuttoned unless so ordered. The traditional "pinch" in the crown is optional but very common.

M-38 *Feldmütze:* early war cap. Three fingers over the left ear, two fingers over the right and one finger over the right eyebrow. The *Kokarde* is centered with the nose. The M-38 should be pinched together at the top, not pulled down so that it looks like a "*feldgrau*–fez!" A safety pin can be used to pin the crown of the hat together, just like they did "back then!"

Schirmmütze (peaked cap): worn square and level on the head with the lower edge even with the eyebrows. The *Kokarde* was to be centered on the face. If you have looked at photos of German Soldiers who are wearing a *Schirmmütze,* you will notice that this is seldom done. Usually, the *Schirmmütze* is cocked over to the right just like the

Feldmütze. Sometimes in fact, it was cocked over and down so far, that one could barely see the wearer's eyes! During recruit training, the German soldier wore a *Schirmmütze* and had it ingrained into him not to touch the bill of his cap. Instead he was taught to hold the cap by the crown. This also comes from the fact that the *Feldgendarmarie* would come down hard on you if there was even a smudge on the brim. This habit naturally was carried over to the *Feldmütze,* and this is actually the reason most soldiers' hats had that pinched look at the top.

Stahlhelm (helmet): to be worn square on the wearer's head and not pushed back, riding on the neck and exposing the forehead. The liner is to be one finger above the eyebrows, with the chin strap firmly in place but not tight enough to cause discomfort.

CLOTHING

Feldbluse (tunic): the proper fit of the tunic should have a collar which would fit two of the wearer's fingers in it. When the wearer sits, there should be no strain on the waist or chest buttons.

Feldhosen (trousers): when worn with ankle boots, the extra material over the calves is pulled inward at the inseam and folded forward before being secured by the *Gamaschen.* Typical fit should be very loose in the legs and will not bind when the wearer does a deep–knee bend.

Schnürschuhe und Gamaschen (ankle boots and gaiters): boots to be proper fit for any outdoor footwear. Should be properly blackened and greased. *Gamaschen* should be worn with buckles on the outside of the leg with the straps pointing rearwards. The bottom of the *Gamaschen* shall cover the top of the boots.

Marschstiefel (marching boots): should fit snugly around the ankle without pinching the ankle and loose in the calf to prevent cutting off circulation.

Mantel (greatcoat): when worn, it is to be buttoned up all the way to the top.

Koppel mit Schloß (belt and buckle): the belt will not sag or hang loose when equipment is suspended from it. The buckle will rest slightly above or over, depending on the size of the soldier, the bottom tunic button. The center of the buckle will be centered with the row of buttons.

EQUIPMENT

Seitengewehr und Koppelshuhe (bayonet and frog): will hang two fingers width to the front of the left rear belt support hook on the tunic.

Patronentaschen (ammo pouches): worn with the inside edges of the pouches in line with the inside edges of the tunic pockets but not more than three finger widths away from the edge of the belt buckle. Again, this depends on the size of the soldier.

Brotbeutel (breadbag): worn on the right rear hip, usually with the right loop just to the right of the right rear belt support hook. The left loop should be in about the center of the back. Again this depends on the size of the soldier.

Gasmaske und Trägbuchse (gas mask can): shoulder strap to be worn over the right shoulder and the belt hook over the rear of the belt in a comfortable position.

Feldflasche mit Trinkbecher (canteen and cup): worn hooked to the right side (front loops) of the breadbag.

Koppeltrugestell (Y–Straps): rear strap to be in the center of the back, hooked to the belt. D–Rings are to be on upper rear of shoulders; O–Ring is to be in upper center of back. Front straps and hooks should be adjusted to fit comfortably and insure that the rear of the straps sit flat. Secondary straps, when not hooked to pack, should be tucked under primary strap and belt.

Zeltbahn (shelter quarter/poncho): strapped to D–rings on the Y–straps, on the *Sturmgepäck* or on center rear of belt. May also be attached to bicycle.

Kochgeschirr (mess kit): strapped sideways, lid to the right, on the *Sturmgepäck* (often seen strapped right-side-up) or strapped right–side–up through O–ring on Y–Straps with an optional horizontal strap that goes around mess kit and rear strap. When worn without Y–straps, the mess kit is strapped onto the left side (rear loops) of the breadbag.

Spaten mit Tasche (small shovel with carrier): for basic impression the *kleines Spaten* is worn on left side of body with bayonet hung between the straps. If using the folding shovel, the bayonet is hung forward of the strap with the scabbard through the loop.

Soldbuch (pay book): habitually carried in the left breast pocket of the tunic.

Erkennungsmarke (dog tag): worn on a cord around the neck, or carried in a private-–purchase pouch, which was also hung from the neck.

Hemd (shirt): the collar on the shirt may be worn outside of the tunic collar only when ordered to be worn that way by the ranking man.

Unterhosen (drawers): there are two loops on the inside of the trousers which slip through the tapes on the outside of the sides of the drawers. In this fashion, the drawers (which do not have elastic in the waist and are not sturdy enough to be held up by buttoning them tightly) are prevented from sliding off the waist.

Socken (socks): worn either under the *Fußlappen* or by themselves. Under garrison conditions, socks with holes are *streng Verboten!*

Fußlappen (foot wraps): worn either over the socks or by themselves. These were favorites of the veterans, some of whom preferred them over socks. Unfortunately, it takes some skill to wrap them around your feet correctly to prevent pressing creases into your flesh.

Aufshiebeschlaufen (shoulder board slides): worn slid over the regular shoulder boards, pushed all the way out to the fold of the board and with the cipher facing away from the soldier.

WEAR OF THE UNIFORM

The manner in which you wear your uniform is also important. To wear it correctly in the field is not enough! When at an event, wandering around the *Flohmarkt* or flea market or socializing, there are a couple of details that you should be aware of. These details can really enhance your impression! The German Army had a number of different uniform dress "orders," which were set by the order of the CO in a "uniform of the day"–type order.

1. *Feldanzug*—Combat gear, helmet, weapon.

2. *Dienstanzug—Feldmütze,* service belt with bayonet. When the event can be construed as being situated "in the Hinterland," shoulder board slides will be worn (if needed).

3. *Ausgehanzug* (walking out uniform)—*Schirmmütze* (if had, otherwise the *Feldmütze*). Shoulder board slides (if needed), *Waffenrock* (dress tunic) if had, otherwise regular tunic. Shooting lanyard. To make this really sharp, do like they did—get a nice second belt, preferably a "patent leather" model along with the same type of bayonet frog. Also, buy a dress–type aluminum buckle and a nice EM dress bayonet to go with this rig, and you will be well on your way to having the *Ganz Prima,* "E–Ticket" *Ausgehanzug.* Later, if you can find one, you can get a *Troddel* (bayonet knot) of the proper color/pattern for your *Kompanie.* A *Schirmmütze* can be purchased, and then you will have greatly improved your impression as a German *Soldat.* So remember, when you leave the barracks to go to the flea market or to dinner (this is at big events only, not at field events), this is the outfit to wear!

4. *Drillichanzug* (work uniform)—German soldiers certainly did not always wear their expensive wool uniforms. Think about this; one doesn't paint buildings or dig ditches in good clothing—that's the way it was then, too—so instead, the *Landser* were issued a cheaper, work uniform originally made of an off–white linen material. Later, this uniform was changed to a *feldgrau* color. Later still, this

was modified into the so–called "reed–green" uniform, which was worn in combat. Though called "reed–green," the color of this uniform was actually a bluish–gray color. These are available as an advanced option for wear by our members for noncombat wear (*Drillichanzug*) and hot weather wear (reed–green uniform).

5. *Sportanzug* (sport uniform)—Black drawstring (not elastic) shorts, white tank–top with sewn–on branch insignia and brown leather running shoes.

Musik!

Mützen u. Stahlhelm
Caps & Helmets

Waffen ᛋᛋ
Schirmmütz

Above, a *Waffen* ᛋᛋ veteran in command of the Axis Forces at FIG 2000 wearing the *Waffen* ᛋᛋ *Schirmmütz* or peaked cap for officers. Metal insignia was authorized, but bullion pieces were used. Branch *Waffenfarbe* was authorized only from May until November of 1940, so it is not historically correct to have a branch color, peaked cap for an officer impression.

A Feldmütz für Offiziere or officer's field cap was introduced in 1934 and served, against regulation, past its wear–out date of April 1942. (Shown on page eight.) Originally issued with woven insignia, these soft–billed caps are found with embroidered bullion insignia. Additionally these caps were found with chin cord added after April 1942.

Waffen ᛋᛋ Schirmmütz or peaked cap for enlisted personnel. Branch *Waffenfarbe* corresponds to shoulder insignia. Only metal insignia is authorized. The black leather chin cord is held in place by black buttons.

Schirmmütz u. Feldmütz
Service & Field Caps

Here, the *Heer Feldmütz* or Army field cap M1934 is correctly positioned at a slant. The *Waffenfarbe* soutache matches the uniform. This cap was modified for use by officers with the addition of silver or aluminum piping and officer grade insignia. This cap was produced through the mid–war period and can be used with any uniform through out the war period.

Ordered modified in July of 1942, the *Feldmütz* or field cap M934 took on a new form with double–button front and fold–down flap. This is a very rare cap, replaced by the *Einheitsfeldmütz* or field cap M1943. This cap can be used with any period uniform in any post–mid–July 1942 impression.

Introduced in June of 1943 the *Einheitsfeldmütz* is one of the German military's best know pieces of headgear. *Heer* caps are of two–button front design. The *Einheitsfeldmütz* was quickly utilized and was nearly universally adopted by the *Heer*. This cap can be worn with any uniform for a post–June 1943 impression.

Feldmütz neur Probe für Offiziere or officer's field cap M1938 differed little from the *Feldmütz* for other ranks and was used officially to replace the officer's field cap by April 1942.

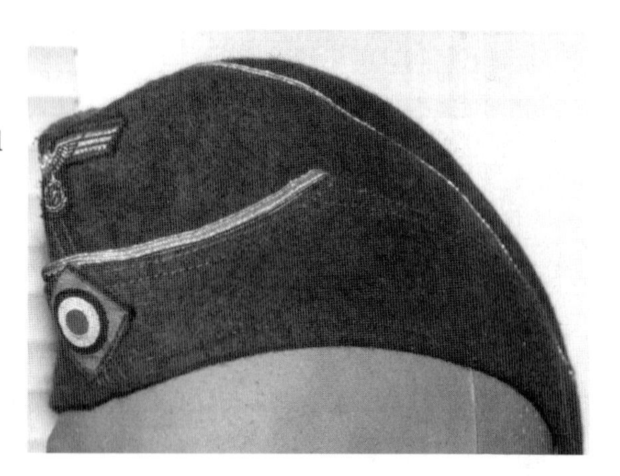

The *Einheitsfeldmütz* or field cap M1943 for officers was available from June 1943 and differed from the enlisted version with the addition of silver or aluminum piping, metal woven or embroidered insignia, and silver–colored buttons. As with the soldier's version, this cap won quick acceptance and can be used with any field uniform in a post–June 1943 impression. This cap did not replace the *Schirmmütz* for non–field applications.

The *Schirmmütz* or peaked cap shown in this photo is piped in gold, has gold bullion insignia and chin cord, and is used by general officers. field grade officer caps had a silver or aluminum chin cord attached by silver–colored buttons and silver–colored bullion or metal insignia. The branch piping or *Waffenfarbe* was the same as on enlisted caps.

The *Schirmmütz* for other ranks makes use of a black leather chin cord and black buttons with silver metal insignia being the norm. The *Schirmmütz* is not an item of wear for enlisted personal outside of the following situations: as *Dienstanzug* or service dress for senior NCOs or for all enlisted soldiers for *Meldeanzug* or reporting dress, *Kleiner Dienstanzug* or undress uniform, *Ausgehanzug* or walking out dress.

The *Bergmütz* or mountain cap is characterized by its short bill and high peak. Patterned after an old Austrian style, this cap was in service from the beginnings of the mountain units. The cap may have either metal or cloth *Edelweiss* emblems and a normally has woven insignia patterned in a 'T' shape. However, the *Gerbrigstruppen* were an individualistic lot, and departures from the norm were frequent. A note for collectors: the *Luftwaffe* had its own mountain–qualified elements used for establishment of high altitude weather collection posts.

Waffen SS Feldmütz neuart or field cap replaced the SS *Verfügungstruppe Feldmütz* in 1940. Branch *Waffenfarbe* soutache was worn on the cap until September 1942. Insignia was in two pieces, woven and sewn to the cap front. This cap can be worn with any post–1940 impression in accordance with regulation, if the soutache is removed.

Waffen SS Feldmütz für Unterführer or NCO field cap was to be worn by NCOs when in vicinity of the *Kaserne.* However, this was a very popular item, and as seen in this photo, it has been modified for use by an officer with the addition of the chin cord. This is historically correct, but outside of official sanction by regulation; the insignia was to be all–metal. However, as the war progressed this was replaced by other types. As most prewar NCOs became officers, this cap would be acceptable with any field impression for the duration of the war.

An example of a private purchase *Waffen SS Feldmütz für Unterführer* with leather bill and woven insignia. An officer in the field could well wear this cap.

Waffen SS Einheitsfeldmütz or field cap M1943 was widely adopted upon issue. This cap shows the early insignia placement on the side and front. This style of cap also was produced in a single–button front style that allowed placement of a both pieces of insignia on the cap front. This insignia combination came woven on a trapezoidal patch. This cap is acceptable with any post–1943 impression.

Waffen ᛋᛋ *Feldmütz für Führer* or officer's field cap was required by January 1940. Insignia is normally of woven metal wire. This cap can be used with any officer impression throughout the war.

Waffen ᛋᛋ *Einheitsfeldmütz* or field cap M1943 for officers was adopted in 1943. Woven metal wire insignia could be placed in either the front/side or the front variation. The cap crown was piped with silver or aluminum. An important note for the collector: while all the examples of the overseas and M43 caps shown to this point have been in *feldgrau,* all the caps that were produced in black for *Panzertruppe* have been reproduced in identical detail.

Stahlhelm
Steel Helmet

The German military used two basic helmet styles during the war period. The *Stahlhelm* shown was adopted for issue in 1935. This helmet was modified with production simplification to the vent grommets, replacing them with stampings in 1940. Either of these helmets is correct for use with any war impression.

In 1943 additional production simplifications continued with the cancellation of the rolling of the edge rim. This gave the newer production helmet a larger and rougher rim. This helmet is only correct with 1943 and later impressions.

Steel helmet camouflaged with rubber inner–tube ring. This expedient method of attaching camouflage is acceptable for all war period impressions.

Whitewash applied directly over the helmet surface is effective. This *Waffen ϟϟ Stahlhelm* displays the runic decal.

Camouflage helmet nets were made from various types of materials and were held in place by a drawstring. This example shows one in place with foliage inserted.

A view of the helmet liner. The *Soldat* has identified his helmet with *Erkennungsmarken Nummer.* Many reenactor units use the last four numbers of the soldier's social security number for this purpose. The "K" may be the man's last initial. Marking all gear, to include the helmet, is a wise idea to aid in return of lost items. Collectors can take the presence of four digit numbers as a suspect point.

A rubber ring holds this winter expedient camouflage. Found from the first Russian winter, this is a historically correct way to camouflage the helmet for snowy terrain.

The *Heer Tarnhelm-uberzug* began to make appearances on the front in early 1942 along with the *Heer Tarnhemd* in the *Splittermuster* or splinter camouflage.

The *Waffen ϟϟ Tarnhelm-überzug* as produced prior to 1942. This camouflage cover lacks camouflage loops. This cover is acceptable for the entire war period.

From 1942 the *Waffen ϟϟ Tarnhelmüberzug* was produced with attached camouflage loops. A note on helmets with decals: double– and single–decal helmets are far more valuable on the collector's market. While many would lead you to believe that postwar decals adhere poorly or look much like the decals on a plastic model, this is NOT true. There are methods to make the postwar decal application convincing. Artificial age also enhances these. Look deeper than just the decal application for clues to a helmet's complete originality.

The *Feldmütz mit Schirm* or peaked field cap worn by this *Grenadier* of *21. Pzr. Div.* is one of many copies made today. In the previous section on uniforms, this same cap with silver cording around the crown and front scallop is shown as worn by officers. This cap preceded the *Einheitsfeldmütz* in design and production. The cap may or may not make use of *Waffenfarbe* soutache. The use of standard boots with *Gamaschen* as well as the use of *feldgrau* wool rank insignia is historically accurate.

Sand–colored paint covered the *feldgrau* exterior of the *Stahlhelm* as shown in this photo of two *Grenadiers* of the *21. Pzr. Div.*

This *Feldgendarm* from *FG Trupp 200* wears the *Tropenhelm* or pith helmet. He is also wearing *Stiefelhose für Unberittene* or breeches for unmounted personnel.

Fussbekleidung
Footwear

Marchstiefel or marching boots, known as *"Knobelbecher"* or "dice shakers" are a trademark item of the German military. Period boots have, as a rule, nailed soles with heel irons as shown in the following photo. Units have varying regulations concerning boot modifications; consult your unit authenticity officer. As new sources are finally producing these in a form that will wear along the lines of the originals, these will become standardized among reenactors.

Clearly shown are the nailed soles of these brand new boots.

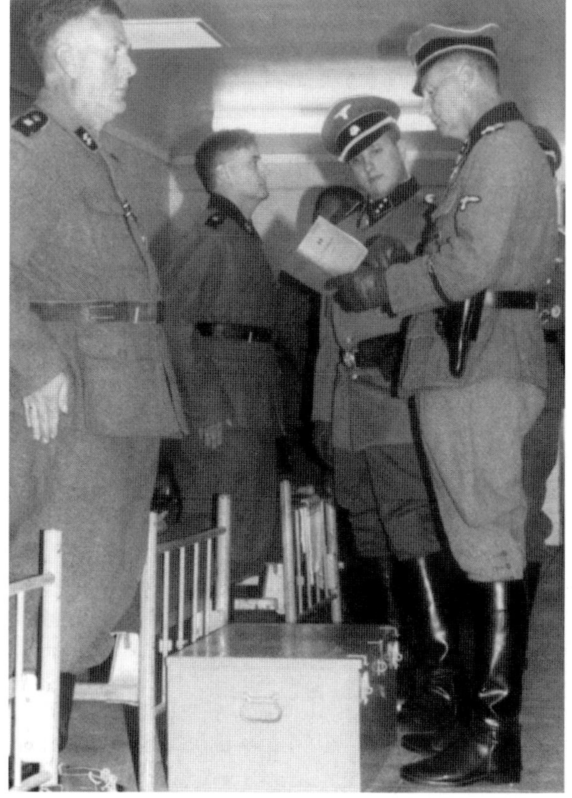

Examples of officer *Hohestiefel* or high boots and *Schnürschuhe* in issue brown leather.

The *Filzstiefel* or felt boots worn as part of the winter uniform.

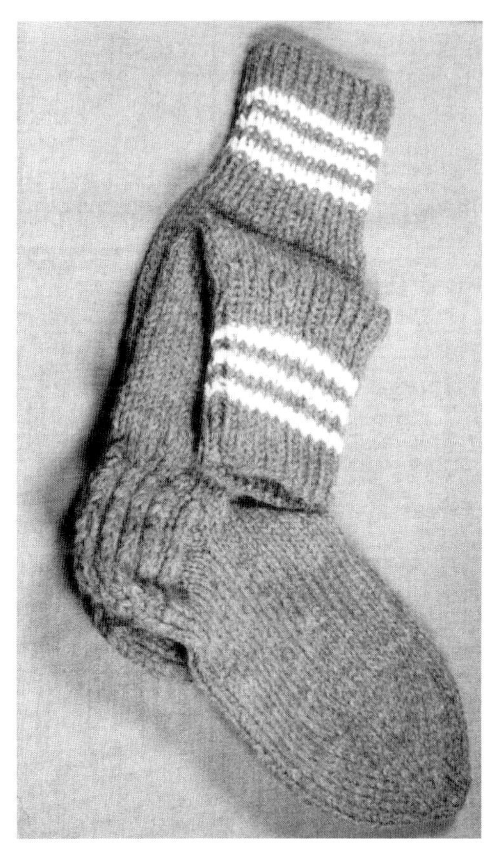

Socken or socks with white size rings—1 ring being small and 4 rings extra large. For the collector, socks are a hard–to–find item. These examples are replicas made by a woman who made them during the war and continues today producing these for reenactors. Factory–made socks are also produced and marketed.

This *Feldgendarm* from *FG Trupp 200* wears *Schnür-stiefel* or lace–up boots.

Pause!

Strickwaren
Knits

Ohren Schutzer or toque can be worn in varying ways. This item is correct with any winter combat impression. Fence wire was often used on helmets to hold foliage.

These *Handbekleidung* or gloves are the standard knit style worn by enlisted soldiers. The rings denote the size, one being the smallest size.

Der alte Hase

By Erich Tobey and Marsh Wise

DER MANN - A *SOLDAT* APPEARANCE

Facial hair was worn in the German armed forces, but with specific regulations applying to all enlisted men. Mustaches could be worn, but sideburns and other exotic facial hair were not allowed. While mustaches were permitted in the German Army, they were rarely worn, as it was simply not in style at this time. In regards to beards—beards were only allowed for *Gebirgsjäger* and then ONLY at high altitudes, only a 2cm growth was permitted.

The truly authentic haircut is shaved from the neck and tapered up to the top of the ears all the way around and slicked straight back (actually worn quite long on top).

This Soldat displays the correct facial and hairstyle of the period. This is actually an Austrian national. Look familiar?

Tattoos—the Germans had them, especially those soldiers from the port cities. If your tattoos have German words in them, good for you. If there aren't any words in them, perhaps you're still all right. If your tattoo says "MOM" or "USMC," keep your shirt sleeves rolled down!

Glasses with non–period frames are really noticeable and detract greatly from the unit impression. Get yourself a pair of silver, round–lens, wire–rimmed frames (available from *Soldat FHQ*), wear contacts, or do without your glasses. If you are going without your prescription eye wear, make sure that the unit commander or your squad leader knows. This would be for your safety as well as anyone else at the event.

Body weight in original photographs show that the men are quite thin. This is mostly due to the wartime diet and the stress of combat. When veterans criticize impressions, the bolder ones will always say, "You are all too fat!"

Age of the German soldier varied. By December of 1943, more than 1,500,000 out of a total of 4,270,000 men in the German Army were over 34 years old. Many of those below 34 were very young (17 to 19) or were recovering from wounds or frostbite. The average age in the whole Army was 31.5 years old. Compare this with the average age for a GI, which was about 26 years old. The average age also varied from unit to unit. For example, the average age of soldiers in the 709th Division was 36. In this division, gun crew ages averaged 45, and some of the men were actually over 55. Generally, though, these older men were placed in support services such as supply or medical and signals units.

Posture is important; shown a picture of a group of German reenactors, a veteran commented, "Look at that! He is standing like an American, slouched with hands in pockets!" Be careful of the typical casual American posture; the traditional German stance is much more upright.

German veterans commented frequently on gum chewing; "Those Americans are always chewing, chewing, chewing, just like cows." In fact, one slang term the Germans had for Americans was „*Kaugummifresser.*" Do not chew gum when portraying a German soldier!

Ausrüstung
Equipment

The *Waffen* ᛋᛋ soldier above drinks from his *Feldflasche* or canteen. The *Trinkbecher* or cup is still attached to the straps. This is the standard issue version of the canteen with brown woolen cover and black leather straps. Cups are found in metal or Bakelite versions. Some units require that soldiers paint their *Erkennungsmarken Nummer* on the cup.

This *Waffen ϟϟ Mann* shows the correct position for wearing the *Koppeltraggestell mit Hilfstrageriemen* or cartridge belt support straps with auxiliary straps. They are attached to the *Patronentaschen* or ammunition pouches, these being for the K98k. He has placed the auxiliary straps behind the others while they are not in use; as soon as he moves they will fall out and hang loosely. These are used to attach to the bottom portion of the *Model 39 Tournister* or pack and the *Gefechtsgepäck* or battle pack. The *Koppel* or belt and the *Koppel-schloss* or belt buckle is correctly positioned at the waist, not riding on the hips.

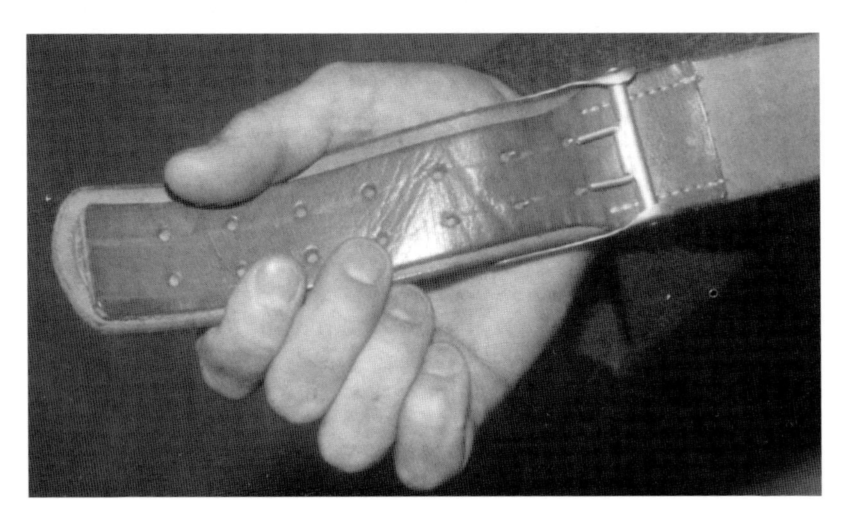

Der alte Hase

Ausrüstung Färbung
Equipment Color

The German military made use of various shades of equipment as the war progressed.

For example most leather used in equipment was dyed black; however, brown was found in some instances such as *Luftwaffe* or as small parts of equipment such as fittings, straps, linings, or reinforcements.

Web used for equipment varied from *feldgrau* to olive to sand. Often colors were mixed on one piece of equipment. Captured or non–German manufacture web was also utilized.

Canvas used for bags was normally olive green, but feldgrau was also used in some items.

Period stitching is usually white. This is lost with cleaning, polishing and dying of leather.

Metal fittings were produced in various metals and painted shades of gray.

Mess kits and canteen cups ranged in color from black to *feldgrau* to late–war olive green. Gas mask carriers were painted *feldgrau*. Units may assign a color for all these items to be painted in a uniform manner with the soldier's *Erkennungsmarken Nummer* added in white.

Opposite: The inside of the *Koppel* showing how the *Koppelschloss* is fitted. For normal wear, the buckle prongs should be fitted into the first (as shown) or second set of holes. The additional holes allow for addition of equipment and clothing items. Not shown here is the leather keeper on the buckle. This flap helps hold equipment on the belt when it is taken off. The flap on the catch end of the belt serves the same purpose.

A rear view of the cartridge belt support straps and the arrangement of basic gear on the belt. The *Tragbüchse* or gas mask carrier is held in place on the belt by placement on the opposite side of the support strap.

The carrier strap passes over the right or left shoulder with the top opening under either arm. This is a unit level decision based on convenience and should be uniform. Likewise the *Brotbeutel* or breadbag is kept from riding around the belt by the placement of the loop opposite the strap. The *Feldflacshe* is suspended on the right hip on the outside of the breadbag by a spring clip. The lower portion of the canteen strap passes through the leather loop on the breadbag and then is reattached to the canteen bottom to keep it from flopping about. The *Gasplane* or gas sheet or cape is strapped to the carrier, the norm in the period of the war when chemical use was not considered likely. Early war impressions show *Gasplane* attached to the carrier strap and positioned in the ready position on the chest.

A well traveled *Kochgeschirr* or mess kit. The soldier's identification number is painted on the lid. A seasoned veteran, he has attached the bail wire under his strap to stop it from making noise. The mess kit often was carried full of food, sometimes soup. In this case it can be strapped in an upright position, and an additional strap may be used to secure it in place on the *Gefechtsgepäck.*

The *Klein's Schanzzeug, Spaten* or entrenching tool is carried in the *Trager* or carrier. The *Seitengewehr und Seitengewehrtasche* or bayonet and bayonet frog or carrier was positioned between the loops of the entrenching tool carrier. The bayonet is held in place by the entrenching tool carrier retaining strap. The *Kochgeschirr* hangs from the *Brotbeutel* by a leather strap with a spring–loaded hook. Like the *Feldflasche* the strap is inserted through the leather loop on the breadbag.

Der alte Hase

Gefechtsgepäck für Inf. Schützenkompanien
Contents of the Infantry Assault Pack

The *Beutel* or bag served as an overflow for items that did not fit in the pockets or the breadbag, yet were desirable to have under combat conditions. The *Reinigungsgerät 34* or standard, weapons–cleaning kit fits into a special pouch sewn into the lid. Other small items such as Iron Rations (small cans of meat and bread), sweater, spare socks, fork/spoon combination, or any number of desirable things were packed in and held in place by the long leather strap that is snugged and buttoned into place.

On top of the full bag, the rolled *Zeltbahn* or shelter quarter with tent pins, poles and rope is strapped down. This covers and hides the bag as well as securing the contents in place in place. The *Kochgeschirr* or mess kit is strapped horizontally at the frame top. There are three metal attaching points sewn into the pack frame. To these the blanket and/or overcoat is attached with straps.

Above, the *Klappspaten* or folding entrenching tool is shown in its *Trager* or carrier. The bayonet is fitted just forward of the carrier, and the bayonet scabbard is inserted through a loop on the lower part of the carrier to hold it in place.
Below, the *Waffen ᛋᛋ Zeltbahn* or shelter quarter is a multi–function piece of equipment. Here it is seen used as part of a tent. Four *Zeltbahnen* are used in one complete tent.

Left: the *Heer* camouflage pattern–*Zeltbahn* worn as camouflage garment. While not rare, *Heer*–pattern *Zeltbahn* have been reproduced. Right: a *Waffen SS*–pattern *Zeltbahn* worn as a camouflage garment. The buttons and mounting rings are easy to see in this photo. *Waffen SS Zeltbahn* have been reproduced in various patterns. Below: larger tents can be formed with the use of more *Zeltbahn*; here is a *Heer* example with eight.

The *Zeltbahn und Zubehör* or shelter quarter and accessories worn rolled and secured to the cartridge belt support straps.

The *Zeltbahn* attached to the battle pack. This pack frame is of total web construction as noted by the web straps holding the mess kit and the shelter quarter.

The *Zeltbahn* strapped to the battle pack. A blanket has been strapped to three rings attached to the frame. This battle pack frame has leather straps to hold the mess kit and shelter quarter.

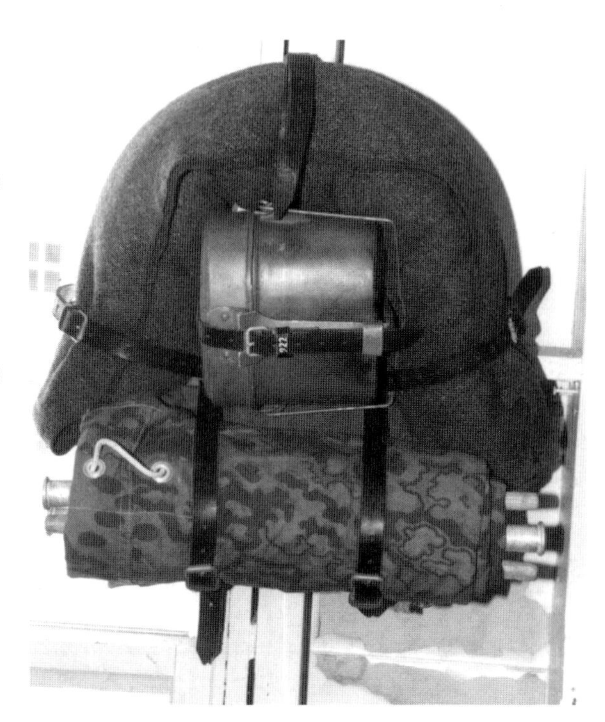

The positioning of the *Beutel zum Gefechtsgepäck* on the frame. Near perfect copies of the frame and pack are produced today.

Patronentaschen G41, G41W und G43 or ammunition or magazine pouches for the G41, G41W and the G43. These are copies of the artificial, ersatz leather version. These pouches are also reproduced in canvas or leather. The normal issue is one pouch per soldier with a standard K98k pouch being utilized on the left side.

Patronentaschen MP43/44 u. StG44 or magazine pouches for the MP43/44 or StG44. These are produced in right– and left–hand sets of various colored canvases.

Patronentaschen MP38 u. 40 or magazine pouches for the MP 38 and 40. Produced in right– and left–hand sets, these have been reproduced for years in excellent quality.

Below, the *Werkzeugtasche 34* or gunner's work tool pouch is a mandatory accessory for the MG34 or 42 gunner. It is carried on the right side. The gunner carries a pistol in holster on the left.

The *Meldekartentasche* or dispatch case is commonly used to carry maps, land navigation and artillery plot instruments.

Brief und Kartentasche or document and map case made with wooden sides, allowing use as an impromptu tabletop.

Doppelfernrohr or binoculars are shown on this officer. On the belt of the officer to the left is the *Behälter* or case for the binoculars.

The front view of the *Piöniersturmgepäck* or engineer assault pack. Explosives, ammunition and gas mask were carried in the side pouches. At the time of this writing, I am not aware of anyone reproducing this item. However, it most certainly will be reproduced as reenacting units strive for more authentic appearance and the price for originals becomes greater than that for copies.

The rear view of the *Pioniersturmgepäck* or engineer assault pack. The pouch in the flap contains the mess kit with more explosive block in the backpack portion.

The *Pionierspaten mit Tasche* is attached to the cartridge belt and the assault pack. The pack attaches to the *Koppeltraggestell mit Hilfstrageriemen* or cartridge belt support straps with auxiliary straps in the same manner as the *Gefechtsgepäck* or battle pack.

The *Rucksack* or rucksack in use. Providing far greater utility than any other type of load–carrying equipment provided by the German military, these were very popular. As with the engineer assault pack, the price of the original has yet to make these viable for replicating.

The *Tragetaschen für Gewehrgranaten* or carrying bag for rifle grenade ammunition has been reproduced as well as carrying bags for hand grenades. The grenade launcher, site tool and grenade are also copies.

The *Feldfunk–Sprecher B* or Field Radio B in use. Interest in use of period communication is growing among re-enacting units, and they are striving to incorporate modern components in period sets to insure function and serviceability.

The *Feldfern-sprecher 33* or Field Telephone being moved forward.

Many larger units are putting entire communication systems into place. This example from *Großdeutschland* makes use of both radio and telephonic communication. Communication impressions require a number of soldiers to lay in, take up, set up and operate the phones.

Tropical field gear includes web *Koppeltraggestell mit Hilfstrageriemen, Koppel,* and brown leather *Patronentaschen.* The *Osterhase* says, " Put your wedding band on your right hand!"

The rear view of the *Koppeltraggestell mit Hilfstrageriemen, Tragbüchse mit Gasplane* or gas mask carrier with gas sheet. *Zeltbahn, and Tropenhelm.*

Tarenanzug, Winteranzug und Schutzanzug

Camouflage Clothing, Winter Clothing and Protective Clothing

The *Schneehemden und Schneehosen* or snow smock and snow trousers. These are white over garments of prewar design for issue to mountain troops. However, they were quickly put into use by frontline units. War period snow camouflage was made of plain white material; postwar *Bundeswehr* snow camouflage has green blotches simulating pine branches in the snow.

A *Panzerkombi* or armor crew overall. These are a rare item now reproduced in various *Waffen* ϟϟ camouflage patterns. Most reenacting units restrict the use of these to vehicle crew members, definitely the use of this item should be checked with unit regulations.

The *Waffen* SS–produced a reversible, padded *Panzer-kombi*. This rare garment was phased out in favor of the *Wintertarnanzug*.

The *Waffen* SS *Tarnhemd* or camouflage smock of the early pattern. While wartime units made use of any pattern of smock, check unit regulations before purchasing.

The *Waffen ᛋᛋ Tarnhemd* or camouflage smock of the late pattern. This style of smock, known as a Type II, can be used in a post–1942 impression. As a warning to collectors: all patterns of *Waffen ᛋᛋ* smocks have been reproduced. When aged and presented with a good story, these are very convincing.

The *Heer Tarnhemd* in its final pattern of cut and camouflage.

Both styles of *Heer Tarnhemd* are reproduced. The first pattern in the splinter camouflage pattern, worn by the soldier on the pillion seat, is one of the rarest of German military camouflage items. These have been made from the correct, bone–white, herringbone twill cloth that gives the appearance that this item is reversible to white.

The *Wintertarnanzug* or winter camouflaged over–uniform. Both the over–jacket and trousers with the snow camouflage exposed.

An over–jacket of the first pattern, gray reversible to white. The double wind flap, waist adjustment, and pocket flaps are clearly visible.

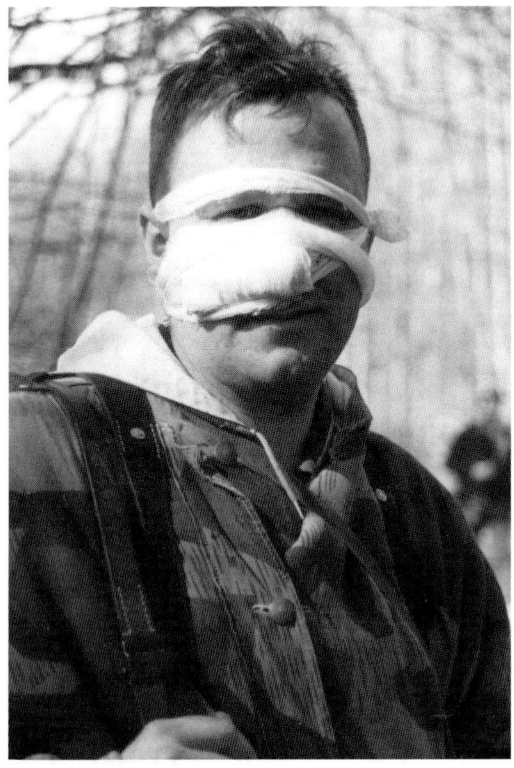

The over–jacket in the *Heer* splinter camouflage pattern. The white side of the reversible hood is visible. Receiving a minor injury early on in the battle, this soldier carries on. Safety is a key part of reenacting; a battle in which none should fall, and wounds should be only theatrical.

Above, *Heer Soldaten* wear both patterns of the over–uniform as they press forward the attack.

This *Waffen ϟϟ* officer wears nearly the complete *Winter-tarnanzug;* all that is missing is the camouflaged pattern mittens. The *Kopfhaube* or padded hood is clearly shown as separate from the hood that is part of the over–jacket.

The final pattern of *Waffen ᛋᛋ* camouflage is used in this example of the winter over–jacket.

Waffen ᛋᛋ Grenadiers advance. They are wearing the *Wintertarn-anzug* with the snow–white camo exposed. The *Grenadier* on the far right wears long *Schneehemden.*

The *Pelzmutz* or fur cap is tied under the chin. These caps have recently be reproduced in both *Heer/ Waffen ϟϟ feldgrau* and *Luftwaffe feldblau.*

The first pattern *Waffen ϟϟ Winteranzug.* Reproduced in pullover and button–up design in either the gray or Italian camouflage, these come in totally fur–lined or semi–fur–lined copies. These were phased out with the introduction of the camouflaged overgarment.

This *Waffen* SS officer wears a *Kradschutzmantel* or motorcyclist's coat. While not reproduced at this point, postwar *Bundeswehr* coats are sold. These have a more olive color to the coat and collar material.

The *Getarnter Drillich-anzug* or camouflaged drill uniform is very popular with *Waffen* SS reenactors. It is worn as part of the uniform (as seen on the left) or as a whole, (as seen on the right). Worn alone, it is a summer–weight uniform. Originals are sought after, and with multiple copies of this uniform being produced in the last ten years, there are plenty that have been "aged" and made available to collectors!

Sized to fit over the wool uniform, as shown in this photo, for cold weather use. When worn as a summer uniform without the woolen uniform, the fit should be baggy.

The *Waffen ϟϟ* produced the first *getarnte Feldmutz* or camouflaged field cap. For a very brief period these caps were issued with insignia sewn to each of the reversible sides. As with any piece of *Waffen ϟϟ* camouflage, the collector needs to proceed with caution. This practice was halted, and caps were produced without insignia.

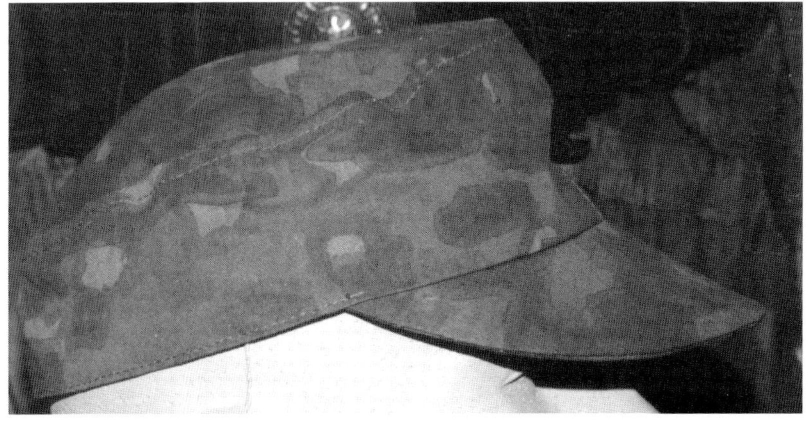

Above, the *Heer* did not produce nor issue any camouflaged caps. However, these were produced privately and in the field. Examples exist in the style shown here or in more of the style of the M43 cap with false sides. These may be encountered with and without insignia sewn in place.
Below, dismounted Grenadiers screen the *Zugmaschine.*

Fallschirmjäger Paratroopers

Above, *die alte Hase—the Zugführer,* and two of his men. All wear thc *Fliegerbluse* with the belt and buckle correctly positioned.

Barracks Identification sign at FIG 2001

A model hair cut and details of the *Fliegerbluse.*

A pause on the barrack's steps shows the *Fallschirmjägerhose* or jump trousers and *Springerstiefeln* or jump boots. Both brown and black boots are acceptable for this impression. The exposed cord on the leg of the *Jäger* at the left attaches to the *Fallschirmjägerkappmesser* or parachute gravity knife. While securely held in a special pocket in the trouser, the cord insured the knife was not lost during a jump. Cords were issued with each knife; however, soldiers often crafted their own from leather or other material, sometimes incorporating artistic design.

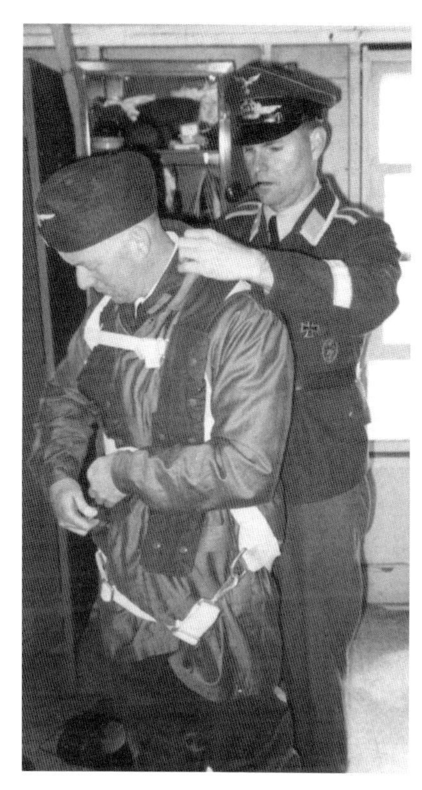

The *Munitionsbandolier* or ammunition bandoleer is adjusted under the *Gurtzeugs zum Fallschirm* or parachute harness. Both are worn over a *Knockensack* or step–in smock. Reenactors made this harness.

Stillgestanden! or attention! *Fallschirmjäger* wore a parachute harness as part of parade dress. Awards and decorations were worn on the *Knockensack.*

Fallschirmjäger-springerhandschue or gloves. These are produced in limited number by reenactors. The cord attaches to the gravity knife carried in the special trouser pocket.

A step–in smock and ammunition bandoleer. Bandoleers are/were produced in both non–camouflage and camouflage types. Replicas are done this way as well.

The *Springer-helm* or paratrooper helmet. These have been produced from GSG9 helmets, cutdown M36 helmets, and from fiberglass and plastic—not a real collector threat. However, now there are at least three firms producing metal replicas. One European model has been sold only as "original" with devastating results! The two US firms offering these have promoted them to reenactors only, but it is only a matter of time until they are "real."

A *Tarnhelmüberzug* with early pattern hook attachment, again reenactor–modified. As with RB stampings the collector will face replicas aged and stamped with *LBA Nr.* or *Luftwaffebauamt Nr.*

A later pattern *Knockensack* in splinter B camouflage pattern. The helmet cover has a drawstring, which is correct for the later issue of this item.

Knockensack come in progressive sizes.

As with the *Heer* and *Waffen ᛋᛋ*, every bit of *FJ*–camouflaged sleeve rank is reproduced. Small FM radios have become popular for command, control and safety in the field; these are slowly being replaced by more period–looking equipment.

The gas mask bag in the ready position. This rare piece of *FJ* equipment is reenactor reproduced. This *Sanitätar* or *"Sani"* has attached loops to his smock for *Signalpatrone* or signal pistol cartridges. The matching *Sanitätstaschen für Unberittene* or dismounted medical pouches are not reproduced but may be repaired or have replica content charts.

The *Sanitätstornister 34* or medical pack Model 1934 is also an original item; however, the medical emblems can be reproduced and added to other packs.

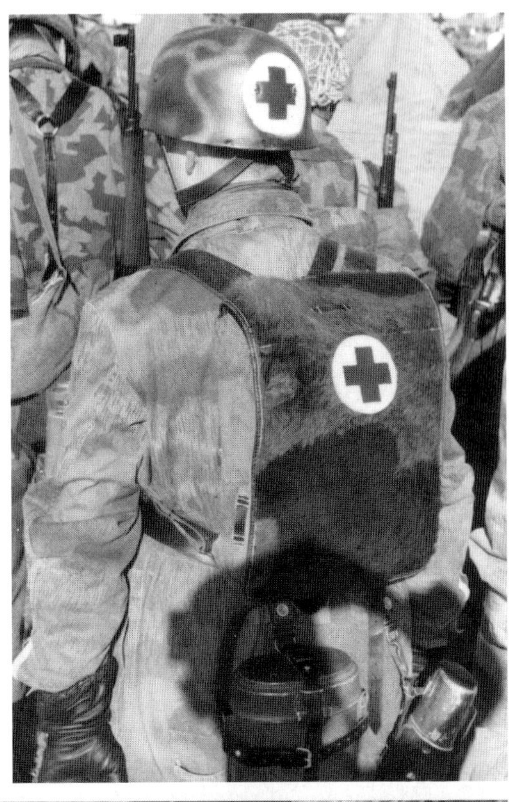

Below, many Communist–period Russian and East European watches are nearly exact visual clones for period German timepieces. The *Sani* uses "blood soaked" bandages to ad great realism to the post engagement period.

Above, tropical uniforms have become popular with German reenactors who are looking for a warm weather substitute to wool. Very convincing *LW* tropical trousers are in circulation now.

Zigaretten? Newly produced packaging holds modern smokes.

Above, planning a move on the objective. Knowledge of land navigation can make or break a reenactor unit during a battle that bases winning and loosing on a system that is in turn based on objectives and time.

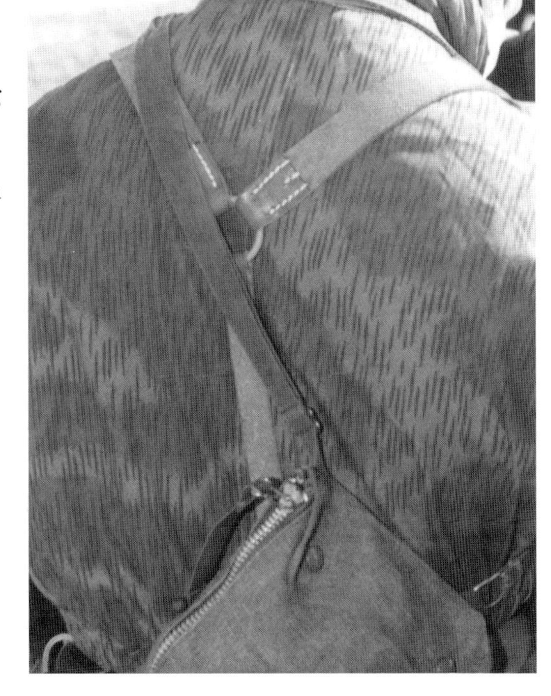

Koppeltraggestell in undyed leather, rough side out. Correct for *FJ* and again reenactor–made.

The use of *Gamaschen* is correct for a late war *FJ* impression. Units control this point of authenticity. This *FJ* also utilizes a normal gas mask carrier, also acceptable for a late war impression.

Below, the *Fallschirm-jägerkappmesser* or parachute gravity knife shown in detail. This is an example of a reenactor–modified *Bundeswehr FJ* knife. The grips have been replaced and the hilt filled, ground and blued. The only obvious giveaway is the postwar blade date or stamp.

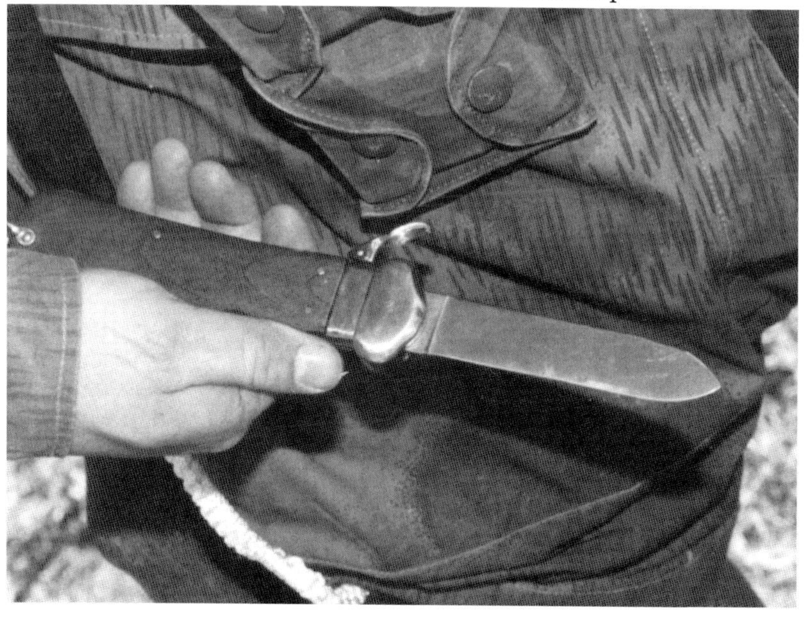

The *Fallschirmjägerkappmesser* or parachute gravity knife in the closed position.

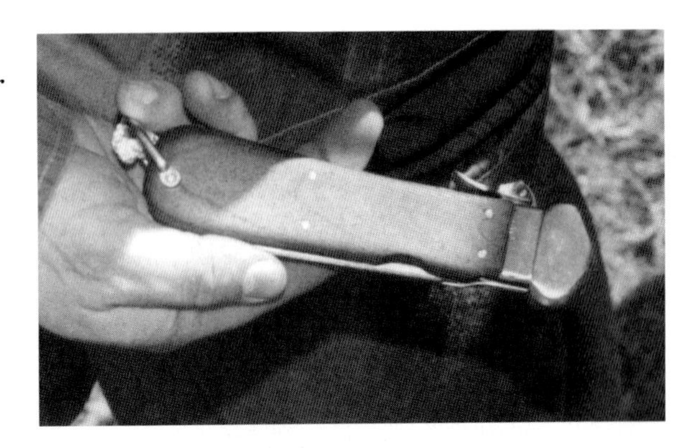

The *Zugführer* uses period binoculars to scan the route of advance. Postwar Soviet binos are near copies except for markings, which can be covered. Just after this photo was taken, the *Zugführer* ordered the attack. Knowing that the route had minimal cover, the enemy was ready and there was a long uphill advance, he was clear that the *Zug* should attack and then "die" well. It is very important to accept "hits" and become casualties, especially in the heat of battle. This is a demonstration of good sportsmanship as well as a great visual for the enemy.

Arrival in a period truck. The German military used German Fords, which are adapted from American models of the same period.

A solid vote for a good event, a tired *Fallschirmjäger* grabs a quick nap after a day in the field.

A true soldier moment—packed in the back of a military truck on a dusty road! Many times agreements with the local National Guard can produce significant support as seen at the TSG National Battle in Atterbury, Indiana.

A very solid *Fallschirmjäger Zug* impression at Atterbury 2000.

Above, another *alte Kamerad,* one of the men I felt good about calling "Sir" in the old days in Germany, Rocco Spencer. Atterbury 2000

A *Jäger* from FJ2 wears the *Luftwaffe* tropical tunic. The helmet has had tan paint applied over the top of the *feldgrau.* This sample is the newest offering of the *LW* tropical tunic. Also available are the *LW* tropical trousers, peaked field cap and shirt, as well as tie.

Gewehr Weapons

Above, *Karabiner 98k* or K98k was the standard battle rifle of the German military. This bolt–action rifle can still be purchased for a reasonable amount, complete with wartime proof marking and manufacture code. German rifles that were used by other countries after WWII may be found at lower prices. There are many Mauser variants; be sure to check with your unit armoror or designate to make sure you are getting the right weapon.
Left, *Gewehr 41* or G41. A rare weapon, this was not a normal weapon for every soldier, and it is important that its use be checked with unit authorities.

Above, *Gewehr 43* or G43 /*Karabiner 43* or K43. Adding a firepower match to the Grand or Tokarev this weapon is correct for later war battles. Not the general issue, use should be checked with the commander. All G/K43s were manufactured with slide rails for the *Zundblickfernrohr 4* telescopic sight. The G/K43 was issued with a single, double magazine pouch and two spare 10–round magazines. The rare *Waffen* SS face veil is a replica as well. Below, the business end of K98k modified to function in the sniper role.

Above, a side view of the telescopic sight mounts. All variants of these mounting systems have been reproduced and when mounted on a rifle, become very convincing to the collector. The lens covers hanging beside the rifle are also new made.

An example of sniper fieldcraft. While reenacting at this time does not lend itself well to the sniper role, the use of an umpire–driven system can make snipers were deadly.

Machinenpistole 40 or MP40, a German military trademark, this weapons provided the German squad with substantial firepower. Each MP40 was issued with two magazine pouches, magazine loading tool and magazines.

Above, *Maschinepistole 43 / Sturmgewehr 44* or MP44/StG44. A selective fire weapon that significantly enhances the German squad. Late–war Tables of Organization and Equipment increased firepower in divisions with fewer soldiers by the use of this weapon. Each weapon was issued with two magazine pouches, loading tool and magazines.

Below, *Maschinegewehr 34* or MG34 was the first general–purpose machine gun. Used either on a bipod or the tripod shown here, the MG34 increases the unit's firepower.

Maschinegewehr 42 or MG42 was a revolutionary offshoot of the MG34, making use of weapons manufacturing techniques and designs still in use today. With a 1,200–round per minute appetite for ammunition, this gun requires a column of ammo box carriers.

The *Gurtrommel 34* or 50–round drum used for assault actions.

This *Waffen ᛋᛋ Grenadier* as an ammunition carrier for the *Zug MG42.*

The MG42's rate of fire required frequent barrel changes, and the *Laufschützer 34* or *42* spare barrel carrier should be in evidence. This weapon became the base of fire for the German infantry squad and had a sythe–like effect in battle. Few reenactors appreciate the power of this weapon as demonstrated by enemy troops that advance into or through its fire.

The 5cm *Leichter Granatenwerfer 36* or 5cm light mortar and other mortars can be modified to fire lightweight charges that add realism to the battle. Strict safety regulations are required for this.

Below, *Waffen ᛋᛋ Grenadiers* pause before the action resumes. The MP40, G/K43s and *Flammenwerfer* make for a devastating assault group.

Above, the *Flammen-werfer 41* or flame–thrower Model 41 in detail. Created from scratch by reenactors, it blasts water, not flames. Only for the dedicated; this is no lightweight toy.

Great way to light your smoke? The view from the front.

Above, in action the *Flammenwerfer,* behind the tree, blasts an allied vehicle and crew with high–pressure water.
Below, hyper accurate *Eihandgranate 39, Stielhandgranate 24, and Stielhandgranate 43* with and without fragment sleeves. The pull igniter has been removed for examination. Handgrenades were not an item that a soldier carried for a long time; they were taken out of their shipping container and used. An authenticity detail is keeping them looking out–of–the–box new.

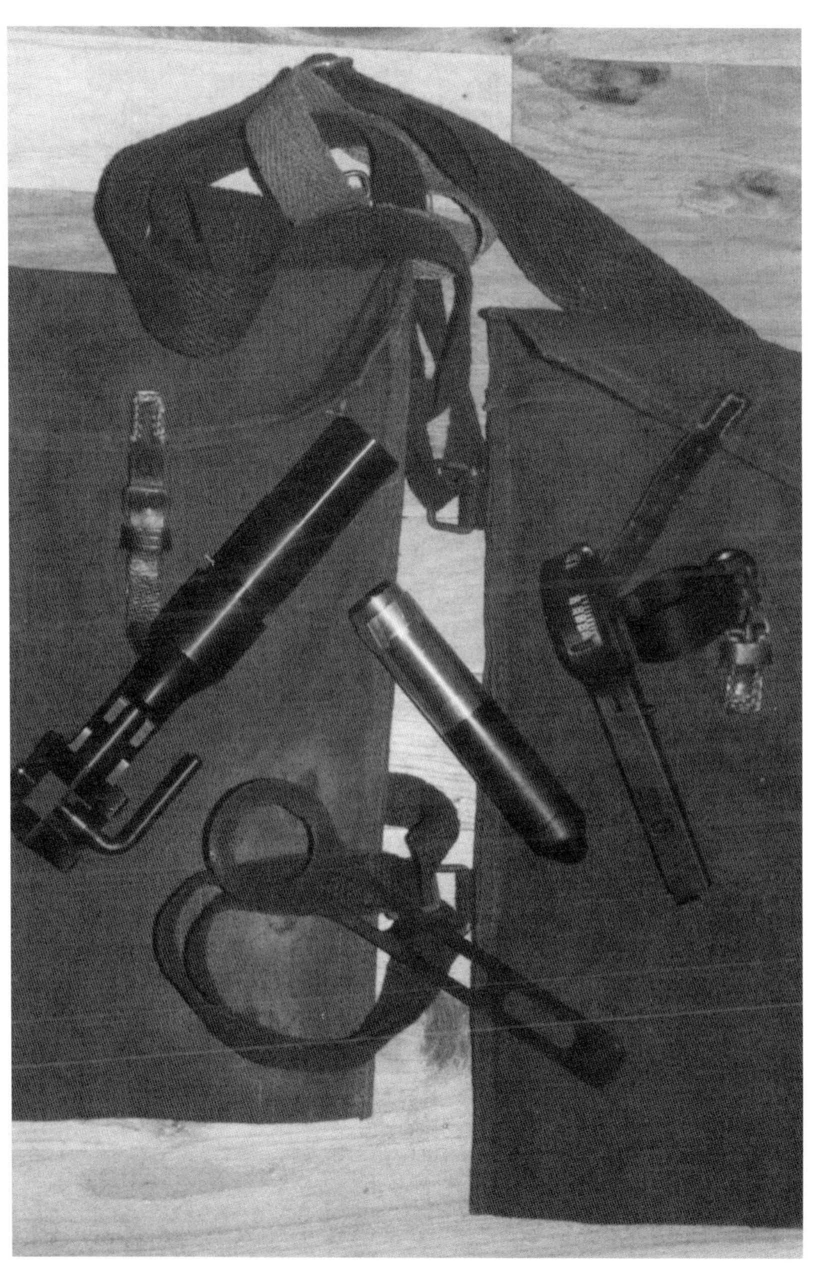

The *Schiessbecher* or grenade launcher assembly. These are completely remanufactured along with various grenades.

Heft Hohladung Granate or magnetic anti–tank grenade.

Heads of the *Stielhandgranate 24* are wrapped around a single grenade to create a powerful blasting charge for use against enemy armor.

Above. the *Panzerfaust 60M* in the firing configuration. Reenactors create these that actually fire a warhead. These must be used in accordance with all safety regulations.

The *Panzerfaust 60M* in the carrying configuration. This is a recently manufactured hyper copy.

The *8.8 Rocket Panzerbuchse 54.* Called the *"Ofenrohr"* or "stovepipe" and *"Panzerschreck"* or "tank terror," this shoulder–fired launcher increases a unit's defense against armor. Late war divisions used these as part of their anti–armor force to make up for the lack of anti–tank artillery. Both modified originals and copies are in use with reenacting units. When firing any rocket–propelled projectile, the use of eye protection is advisable and safety regulations must be adhered to.

Young Grenadiers watch for Jabos.

An dem Kaserene und in Zeltlager Personal Items, Barrack and Field Impression

No doubt which unit is your host. *Großdeutschland* at the Fredrick Airshow 2000.

For a first–class impression, the paperwork is never done! From the individual *Soldbucher* to the roll of *Toilettpapier* in the barracks, there is always one more benchmark to strive for. As WWII reenacting grows and matures, the attention paid to the details of life in the *Kaserene* and *Feld* increases. The following are some benchmarks reached by 2000 by Großdeutschland, *LSSAH, 3. PZG., SS –"Deutschland"* and *FJ Rgt 6.* For the collector, the warning here is that nothing is beyond the grasp of the reenacting artisan and therefore not beyond the reach of the fake monger!

Ammunition cartridge boxes, razor blades, match boxes, moleskin and batteries in period containers offer the unit member options to make his impression far more complete.

Boot laces and polish help fill the unit kanteen

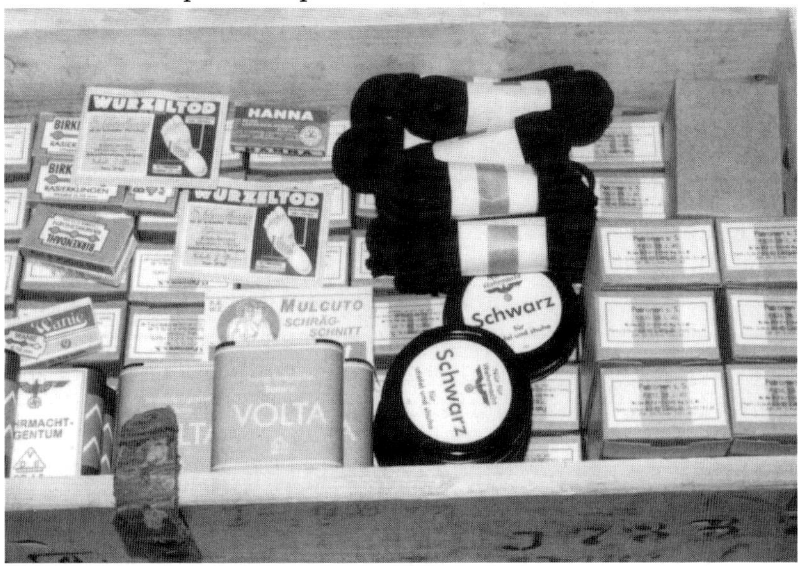

Period–looking boxes for the *Eisbit Kocher und Troken-Brennstoff* or the *Eisbit* individual cooker and dry fuel tablets.

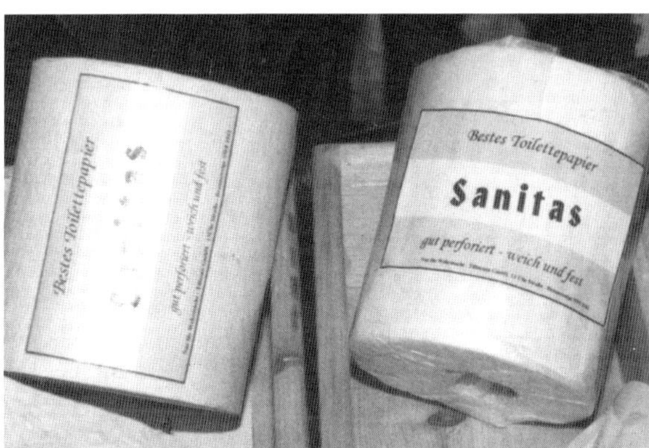

Toilettpapier.

Above, a necessity in the barracks of modern day. As every soldier knows, secure your uniform and equipment. This period style lock makes the job look right.

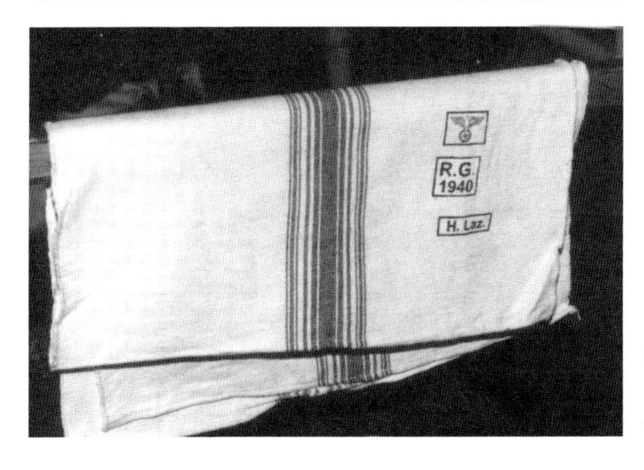

A towel marked as property of an Army Hospital.

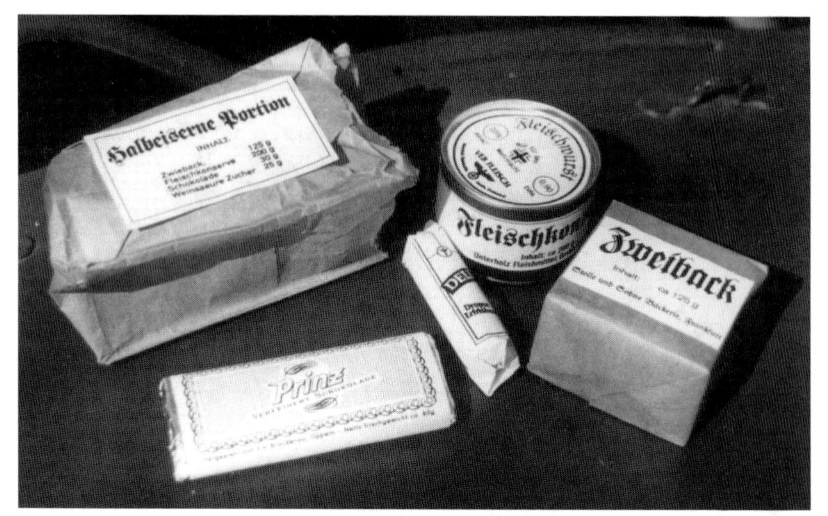

While not historically correct in shape, construction nor content, this *Halbeisern Portion* is far more at home with the period German impression than modern food. This packet is designed to feed one soldier; on this day it fed three.

The exterior detail of the *Halbeisern Portion* package with list of contents held in hand for size comparison.

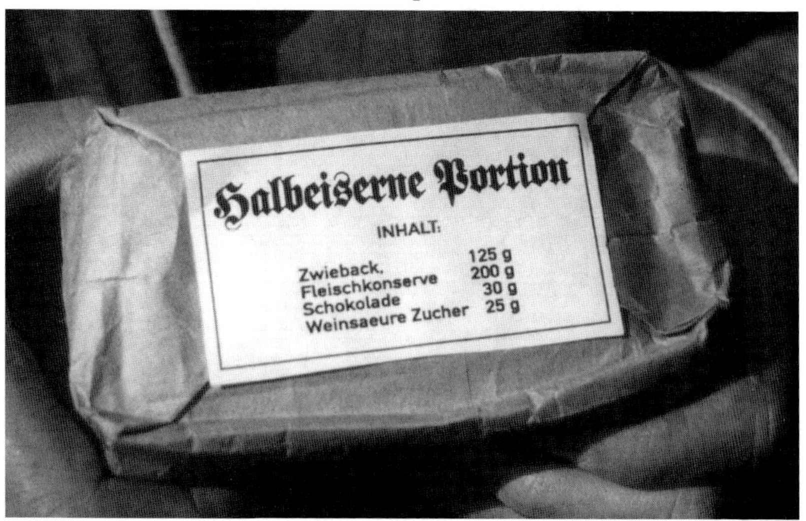

Der alte Hase

Der Mann - A Guide to the Persona
By Marsh Wise

What is your persona?

A persona is the period character the reenactor takes upon himself while at events; it is a period alter ego. A lot of reenactors either don't know where to look, or can't think of who they want to be. Researching a persona is not that hard, it just takes a little time and research. This *alte Hase* will help you to build your persona and also to give you a good foundation for acting it out.

Who are you?

The first item that you come to is your German persona's same. This is usually one of the very first things a new *Rekrut* does, and hopefully you will pick a good authentic, period, name for your persona. If you're having trouble with this, here are some guidelines.

Your persona name can be your own name (if it is of German extraction), the name of a relative or any German name that catches your fancy. A way to honor someone who fought in the war would be to pick the name of a German soldier, perhaps, from our unit who was killed in WWII.

Do not pick the name of someone such as "Sgt. Steiner" from *The Cross of Iron*—nor should you make your last name Bismarck or some other BS like that. This is considered "cheesy" and will only end up getting you taunted. Another thing about your German name—it should not have a *„von"* in it! Unless you are of the nobility and are an officer, you shouldn't have a *„von"* in your name! Just because every single WWI or WWII movie ever made has a German with the name *„von“* Somebody–or–other in it, does not mean that you should be a *„von.“* Nobility generally were not enlisted soldiers, they went off and got to be officers. Usually, about the ONLY way a *„von“* would be enlisted, was for a major infraction and being a disgrace to his family!

What is your social class?

What social class do you come from? Then, like now, there were different classes in society. Although this is not such an admirable custom, and even decried by the Nazi Party, it was one which was very much still in existence during WWII Germany. The Germans call this *Stände.*

Where is your home?

To this day in Germany, as in the US, there is lots of "Home Town" pride. If you're from the north or south, you usually let others know it; even if you don't, many little things (the way you speak, the clothes you wear, mannerisms) give you away. It was the same "back then." Choosing a town or city is relatively easy if your unit knows their background, as *Heer* units were recruited from geographic areas inside the *Wehrkreis* system. *Waffen–SS*, *Luftwaffe,* and *Kriegsmarine* recruited on a national level. Get an old map of Germany, from before 1945. My advice is that unless you have some kind of heartfelt attachment to say Berlin, Breslau, München or some other big city, pick a small town or village. Anyway, go ahead and pick one! Then to do this right, try and get a more detailed map of just that area (or even the town) you want to be from. I have a nifty book called *Städte–Atlas Schlesien.* This book consists mostly of old street maps of cities in Schlesien right before and during WWII (There are also such books available for Preußen, Pommern and Posen.) So, voila—you can now find your address!

When is your birthday and how old are you?

Okay, now that you have a home, when were you born? This is pretty easy; simply subtract you current age from 1943, and this is the date you want to be born on. Of course you can pick another date than your own birthday, but it's easier to remember. A note on this: you might want to add a couple years or so to your age so as to not grow out of your impression.

How large is your family?

Now, think about your family. Are they still alive? Who is your father and what are his interests? Most Germans have a formal profession; what is *Vattis?* How about *Mutti;* what was her maiden name? Does she do war work? Are you married? If so, make up a good German name for your *Frau*. Go for it; I'm sure she'll be thrilled with your choice. Any *Kinder* (kids)? If so, "German–ize" their names. Next thing, if you were born around 1920 or later, you were probably in the *Hitler Jugend* (Hitler Youth), especially true for *GD* members. This could provide another dimension to your impression, i.e. HJ Leader, etc. You might want to spend some research time on this.

What is your profession?

Now, what is your peacetime profession? You can have fun with this or simply use the equivalent of your modern job. If there is no equivalent, try and match it to some period profession. Were you an engineer, a salesman, laborer? Farmer would be good, as would a student. Or perhaps you are a factory worker, teacher, lawyer or ditch–digger (There you go, that last one fits you!) Oh yes, you most probably also spent a year or so in the *Reichs Arbeits Dienst* (RAD) before entering the Army. This was done not only to "toughen up" the new *Rekrut*, but also gave the government a labor pool to build things, help repair air raid damages, etc.

Did you fight in WWI or join the *Sturm Abteilung?*

If you are older, did you participate in WWI? If you were born before 1903, it's a distinct possibility that you have fought for the Fatherland before. If you do decide that you were a veteran, then you need to ask: Where? With what unit? Also: "Was I in the Sturm Abteilung (SA)?" A lot of WWI vets were, as the SA was a popular veteran's organization. Another popular veteran's organization was the *Stahlhelm* organization.

Were you drafted?

After Hitler repudiated the Versailles Treaty, German men were once again eligible to be conscripted for military service. When were you called up? Did you voluntarily return to service after the war started, or did you force the *Kettenhunde* to come and drag you away?

Act out your persona with conversation.

While scenarios are underway, try to maintain a "first person" impression. Talk about period topics and concerns, carry out period activities, and act like it is "1943" (as much as possible). You should try and speak German as much as possible or at the least use an accent (more on this later). You don't have to do these things all the time, but when in a period situation (when an attack is underway, you are bringing in a prisoner, etc.) do your best to play your part as a German *Soldat.*

Remember the *Landser* did not always talk about his uniform, equipment or weapon. To him, these items were part of his job, not a hobby. Would you like to think about, talk about or even be reminded of your job all day, all the time? Of course not, then just like now, soldiers wanted to try and escape from their "job," that's why they pursued other amusements.

Act out your persona with hobbies.

What are your hobbies? Don't say reenacting, it didn't exist then. Perhaps you like music, politics, sports, photography, or going to the movies? It's possible you just like to read; this was quite popular in the olden days—you know, before TV. Possibly you are a poet! Maybe you traveled before the war, possibly even to America. Whatever your persona does, try and make it something that you enjoy now; something you have knowledge about (or barring that, something you feel like studying). These are just a few of the details which you should think about.

Use the German language.

When trying to maintain historic accuracy in the presence of Soviet, British or even American troops, members who speak no German are asked not to make loud conversation in English and to, in general keep usage of the English language to a minimum. Familiarize yourself with the German words for parts of his uniform and equipment, as well as the most common military terms *(Schützengraben, Hande hoch, Stellung, Hinlegen, usw.)*. Another *alte Hase* contains Level 1 German, and numerous other items are dual captioned in German and English to help you.

Try an accent.

If you cannot speak German or when English speech is necessary, it has been found that the use of an accent can be quite effective and greatly reduces distraction. Using an accent will also put people in a much better mindset rather than trying and create a German dialog or conversation. Although some reenactors are against this, the use of a German accent (especially if you don't know much

German) can really be effective. Speaking with a German accent will add a lot to your impression, just as buying a good uniform, boots and a rifle will. Sometimes when you first try using an accent, people will think you're strange, but if you persevere, eventually it will catch on with them too.

To be effective though, an accent can't be goofy—like some actor in an old WWII movie or Sgt. Schultz in Hogan's Heroes; "Vell, vell Col–o–nel Hogan, Vhat do you tink I am, an eediot?" Instead of this, simply pronounce some of the letters as a German would; Especially the "W" as a "V" and the "J" as a "Y." Reinforce this with the addition of German words interspersed throughout your conversation.

Nothing appears more ridiculous an otherwise authentic German soldier yell out "Hey, German guys! First squad with me, second squad with Joe. Everyone fall in at left–shoulder arms." Instead, how hard is it to say, *„Achtung, Deutsche Soldaten! Erste Gruppe with me, Zweite Gruppe with Gefreiter Schmidt. With Stahlhelms—Angetreten! Mach schnell! Das Gewehr—über!"* Doesn't that sound much better? Of course it does, it was in what I call "Pidgin–Deutsch," which anyone can do! Most of us could figure out what was just said there—especially with a little practice and study. STOP calling it a helmet, it's a *Stahlhelm.* And, you don't have a gun or a rifle— it's a *Gewehr.* Soon, you'll be using these words without thought, much like most of us already do with the word *Zeltbahn.*

Waffen ϟϟ Feldgendarmerie

Papier! With a correct impression comes research and work on who you are, where you have been and what you have done. There is a place for everything.

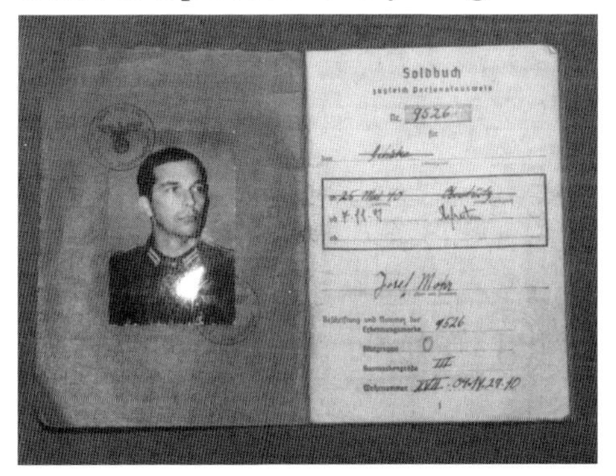

The *Soldbuch* or repository of all the information a German soldier carries about himself on himself.

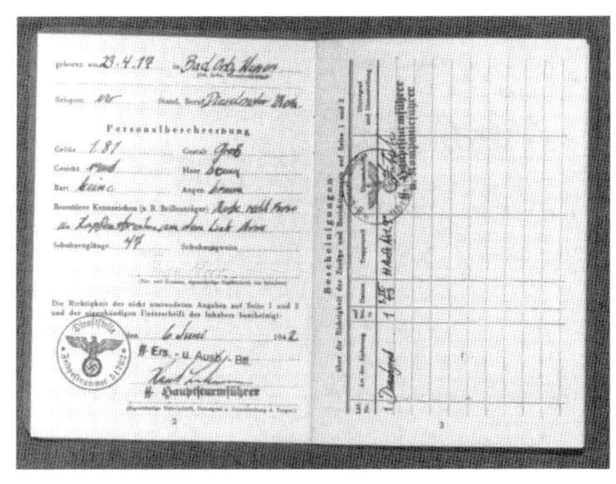

A correctly completed *Soldbuch* is in the higher levels of authenticity, just after the use of the German language.

The *Soldbuch,* photos, documents and other stuffers tell a personal story of the soldier.

Reichsmark, a tangible proof of service. Send it home or loose it on *Skat!*

Above, step through the door and back in time. The goal of a successful barrack impression as mastered by *Großdeutschland.*

Individual item and signs arranged to produce a period feel.

Above, the *Kompanie Schreiber* or company clerk at work.

Tagesbefehl or daily order or schedule. Where to be and when!

The overall barrack impression.

Der alte Hase

Kaserne und Biwak
Barracks and Camp
by Erich Toby and Marsh Wise

The prewar German soldier spent most of his time in the *Kaserne,* but even the late–war recruit spent enough time there to become familiar with the nuances of *Wehrmacht* barracks routine. The following are some of the more important concepts for the reenactor to know.

German soldiers were quartered together in a room called a *Stube.* The number of men in the room varied according to the size of the room, but 6 to 12 would have been typical. The *Stube* had three common furnishings:

- lockers—these were called *Schranke,* and they were similar to a wardrobe; they were issued one per man.
- a table for the occupants of the *Stube* along with a number of backless chairs, called *Schemel* which were issued one per man.
- bunks or beds.

Whenever possible, we will use the following standard for filling our lockers: all non–period or non–authorized gear will be stored elsewhere, i.e. in your vehicle!

For training, the recruits from a number of rooms were organized together in a *Korporalschaft.* A drill instructor (usually an *Unteroffizier*) was assigned to each *Korporalschaft.*

One man in each room was assigned as the *Stuben-alteste,* or room elder. In a regular army unit, this man would have automatically been the senior *Gefreiter* or, lacking *Gefreiter,* the private with the most service time. For trainees, he may have been the oldest recruit, the first man in the room, or he may have been chosen at random.

The *Stubenalteste* was given the responsibility of insuring the *Stube* was clean and orderly, that cleaning details were parcelled out, news was disseminated, etc.

In the German Army, the "officer of the day" was an NCO and was called the *„Unteroffizier von Dienst."*

Common occupations while in the *Kaserne* included *Unterricht* (instruction), *Revierreinigen* (housekeeping), *Waffenreinigen* (weapons cleaning), *Putz-und-Flickstunde* (repair and cleaning of uniforms and equipment), and *Appell* (inspection).

The evening retreat in the German Army was called the *Zapfenstreich.*

For events which have barracks, we may implement some or all of these activities. At the very least, you will need to bring the following to a barracks event:

- one blue and white checked blanket sack
- one blanket (the standard unit one)
- two flat sheets, white
- one blue and white checked pillowcase (or at least a plain white one)

A German field camp is a *Biwak* (bivouac), and was commonly set up from various sorts of tentage, usually including the small *Zeltbahn* (tent). Made of four *Zeltbahnen*, this will sleep three men, the owner of the fourth *Zelt* being on duty. *Zelts* could also be buttoned together in different combinations to make larger tents.

Schrankordnung (Locker regulation):

- Clothing will be hung in the locker with buttons facing to the left; this exposes rank chevrons.
- The clothing will be hung with the heaviest garments on the left, the lightest on the right. For example: from left to right, overcoat, spare tunic, HBT tunic, shirt.
- The *Tornister* (rucksack) is placed on top of the locker on the left; the gas mask cannister stands on end on the right with the helmet on top of this.
- Personal effects and other items are stowed per direction of the Administrative NCO.

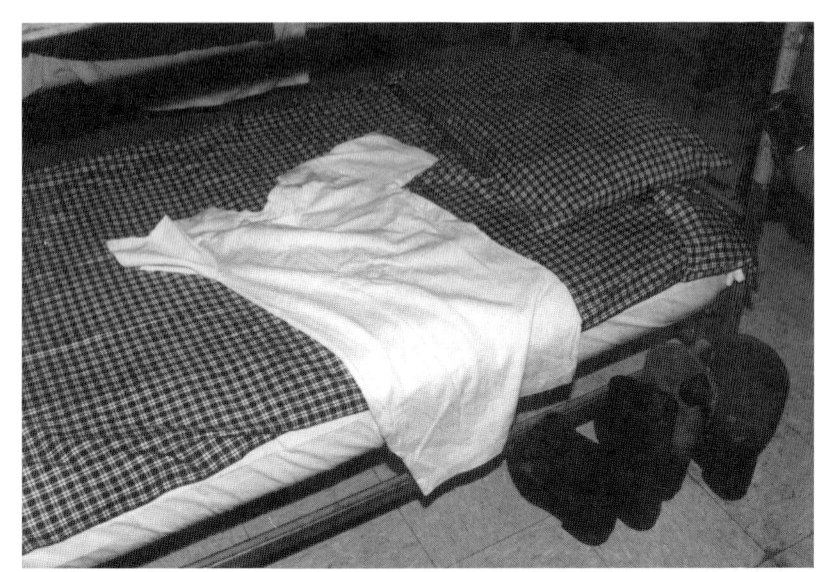

Above, details of bedding which puts the GI bunks in a whole new perspective. Bedding is the unit requirement that provides this level of authenticity.

Each *Soldat* had a stool and name on his bunk. The hung gear would be unacceptable in the pre–1945 barracks. The equipment gives more flavor to the impression. Unsecured equipment is a target for theft.

American military lockers can be made to look reasonable. Some units are now making wooden lockers to German wartime pattern. Wood or metal hangers only!

The unit cipher in stained glass.

The traditional *Weihnachtsbaum und Geschenk* or the Christmas tree and presents.

The *Großdeutschland* Christmas Celebration and the arrival of the *Weihnachtsmann und Ruprich.* A time of levity and joking followed by *Bierzeit. Fröhlich Weihnachten!*

Impressions are not just in the barracks as *L⚡⚡AH* shows during an awards ceremony. Numbers are impressive and recognition of loyalty and work essential!

Fresh from the battle, the *Kommandeur* awards his *Soldaten.*

Barracks's Inspection with all gear and uniforms displayed. Another way to make any barrack feel like *Heim.* While this is obviously a modern, US building, the work done helps suspend the reality. The placement of the bag on the assault frame is not correct.

Any use of period equipment and gear help with the barrack impression. Any soldier who has ever arrived at any temporary barrack knows it will be Spartan and without character, something soldiers quickly change as they adopt their new surroundings.

A unit sign next to the entrance desk.

Below, the fun of being a German reenactor has overtaken this young SS–*Mann!*

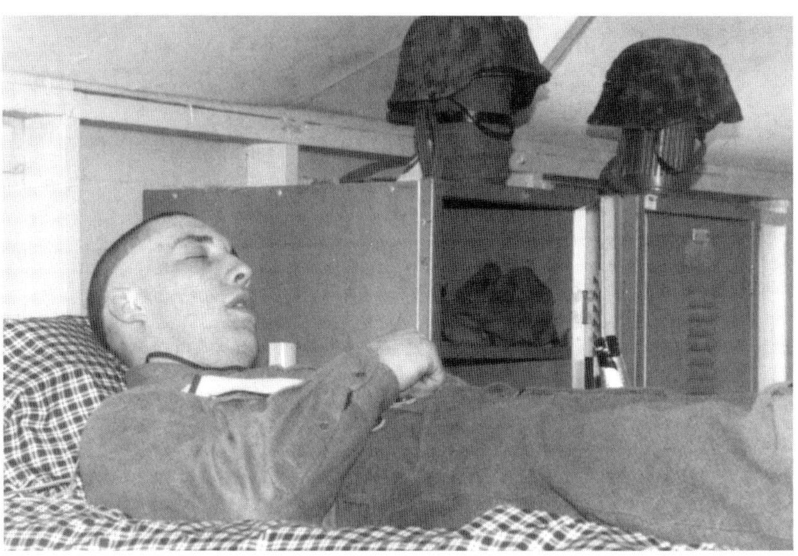

The barrack of *3. Panzergrenadier,* the author's FIG hosts. The use of nameplates stools and uniform bedding along with spots of gear and posters make this a very acceptable barrack impression. Any unit can achieve these standards with quality leadership and determination. Of note: the *Ostihausstiefel*

Strong units have things in common beside visionary leadership. One is the use of food. *GD* makes use of a field kitchen to do this in a very authentic manner. "An army marches on its stomach" is the noted quote. The reenactor is no

As with any food preparation the cook is hard at it all the time. His reward is that of any military cook; he watches it go down and takes a request for a second helping as thanks!

Der alte Hase

Ersatz Schmaltz

Soldaten can make *Ersatz Schmaltz* from the following recipe:

Ingredients:
1/4 lb. Lard *
1/2 medium cooking onion, chopped fine
1 tbls. chopped chives, fresh or dried
1/2 tsp. garlic powder
1/4 tsp. salt
Purchase a block of lard (usually sold in 1#–blocks) in the fresh meat department. Take half of a medium sized yellow (cooking) onion and chop it up fine. Sauté the onion in a small bit of margarine in a small skillet until it is turning golden brown. Set the onion aside. Melt approx. 1/4 lb. of lard in the same pan. When it is liquefied, stir in the onion, garlic powder, salt and chives. Mix thoroughly and place the pan in the refrigerator to cool. After about an hour it will begin to congeal. Stir it thoroughly to mix the ingredients again (the onion and chives will have settled to the bottom) and spoon the mixture into your *Fettdose.* Allow it to cool overnight in the refrigerator. This makes about enough for 1-1/2 *Fettdosen.*

* *Gans Fett* (Goose fat) is a bit hard to come by; substitute Schwein Fett (hog fat) or "lard."

Danke, Rich!

Above, *„Hunger ist die beste Koch"* is an old German phrase I saw in a mess hall, but this was *„spitzen klasse Futter!"*

Another unit enhancement is *Kameradschaft* or doing things together. The *Schuhmacher* works as he talks with *der Hauptmann* and other *Großdeutschen.*

All the comforts of home in the command tent, complete with period style bedding.

The place plans are made.

Zelt für Offizier.

Part of the *GD Zeltlager* at the Fredrick Air Show 2000

Below, aircraft warning sign.

Unit direction signs. The girl beneath the lamp catches the passerby's attention. Other unit signs give FIG 2001 visitors a real eyeful! *Großdeutschland* supported a superb public display at this event.

The *Entlausungsanstalt 65* indicates the way to the delousing station! St. Vith was a key, crossroad town seized early in "Watch on the Rhine" by the *Führer Begleit Brigade,* a unit that grew out of *Großdeutschland* expansion to a *Panzerkorps.* (See *SOLDAT Volume V.)*

The way to the field latrine and the movie house!

A small tent made from Italian camouflaged material used in a DAK scenario.

Food, comradeship, service, high expectations and standards build relationships. It is strong relationships that makes for a cohesive, happy, and thriving unit.

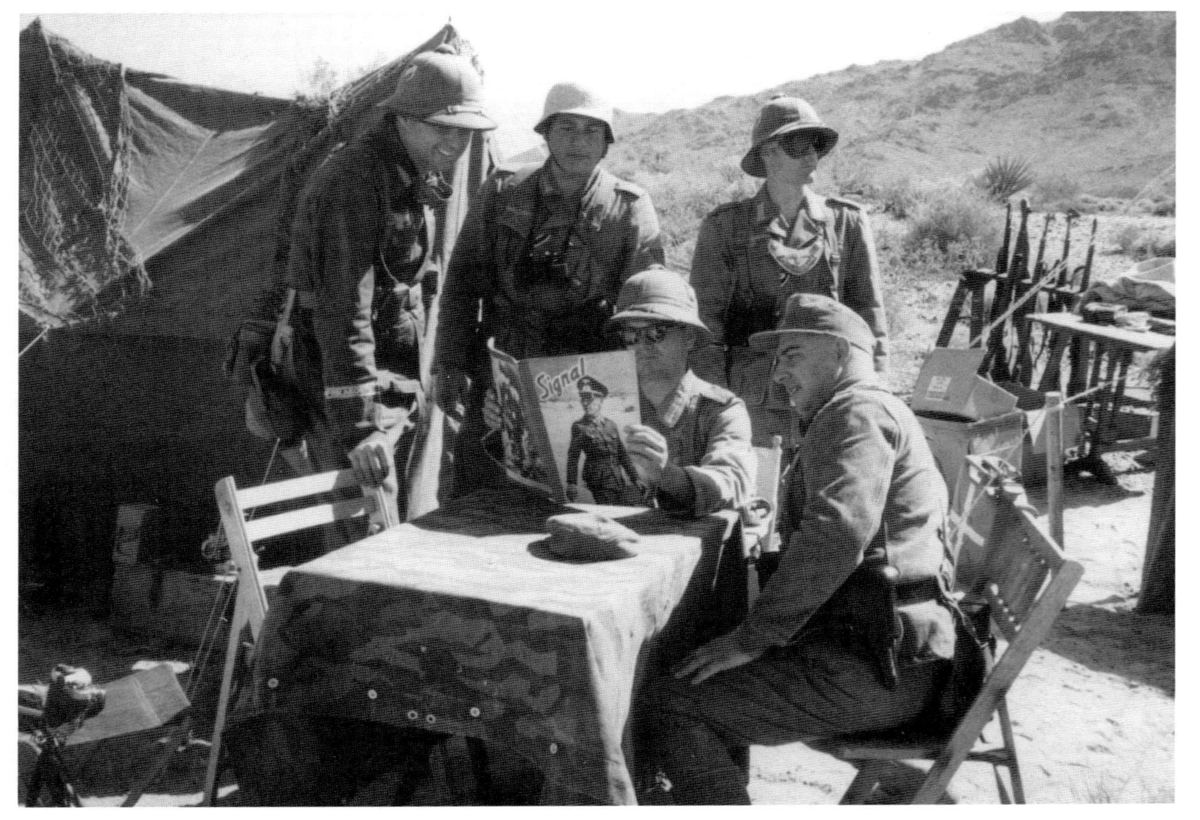

"So, that is what we are up to!" *Grenadiers u. Feldgendarm* catch up on the news from *Signal* magazine while at camp in a California based DAK battle.

Der alte Hase

Der Mann
Germanic Mannerisms and Cultural Traits - A Guideline for First Person Impression
By Marsh Wise & Erich Tobey

Willi Hellpach, a German writer, compiled what he termed the "six positive characteristics of the Germans. The following traits are more or less valid for Germans in general.

Creative Energy

On a large scale, the Germans have always been great builders and inventors. On a smaller scale, individual Germans are some of the world's hardest working people. In fact, another German writer named Hermann Eich expressed the negative corollary of this trait; "The Germans have a mania for work. They have no idea how to enjoy life." GIs who occupied German positions were amazed to find bunkers with screen doors, carpets, paneling, and flowers on the table. In other German camps, the *Landser* had been raising gardens and had small rabbit farms. German prisoners even made working model trains from wood. Germans have a reputation of being diligent and creative workers. Germans are seldom idle, so remain in a state of being busy improving positions, repairing uniform or equipment, checking paperwork, writing letters, etc.

Thoroughness

The Germans have a much used saying: „*Wenn schon, denn schon.*" In English this means that if something is worth doing at all, it is worth doing right. It seems that the Germans never do something halfway. They are masters of organization and give great attention to detail. The negative implication here, of course, is that they are perfectionists and fussy—the perfect trait for the ideal bureaucrat, who appears again and again in German literature. *„Wenn schon, denn schon."* It would be tough to improve on this. Take the time to develop the smaller details, like emulating the traits found here: developing a persona, issuing paperwork, procurement of personal effects, etc. Strive to perfect the unit, so that it works for the benefit of not only members but also the hobby in general.

Orderliness

Here's another famous German saying: *„Ordnung muß sein!"* (There must be order!) Germans are neat, and everything must go by the rules. Punctuality is another byproduct; the trains are always on time, and woe to the person who is late for a meeting with a German! Of course, this mania for order also had some bad side effects. History shows that German soldiers during both World Wars reacted with unreasonable ferocity when occupied peoples did not "play by the rules." Stick to the rules. Keep camps, billets, and persons neat and clean. Don't tolerate sloppy or ill–maintained uniforms and equipment. Do not accept disruptive behavior. Always be punctual.

Sincerity

Germans pride themselves in their honor; they generally do what they say they will. Even Adolph was quite frank when he told the world what he had planned in his book *Mein Kampf.* On the other hand, there is another famous quote: "A German never tells a lie unless he believes it." It appears that sincerity can also be interpreted as "blue–eyed self–righteousness." Be true to your word, pay your debts, and be honest with one another.

Firmness

More tangible terms might be "persistence," or "single–mindedness." More accurate might be the terms "bull-headed" or "stubborn"—take your pick. Willi Helpach was German, so he chose the more attractive term of, what can you expect, loyal.

Loyalty

Here is a trait, which the Germans have developed almost to the point of self–destruction. The *Waffen-ϟϟ* even had as its motto *„Meine Ehre heißt Treue"* (my honor is my loyalty). Loyalty to his organization, family, country, and comrades is one of the things that makes the German a natural soldier. However, at various times throughout history, the Germans have developed loyalty to its negative extreme: fanatical nationalism. Combine this with "firmness," and you got the stereotypical German would tell you that Germany, and the Germans were superior, no matter what you said.

Song

Germans like group singing. To Americans, singing often seems overly sentimental or corny; singing of patriotic tunes is considered especially trite. To the 1940s German officers, a lack of singing was an indication of bad morale. It is surprising just how much this aspect of German military life is neglected by reenactors, despite its authenticity and relative cost—nothing! Learn some of the marching songs and sing them! It may feel awkward at first, but it is important, and the more unit members who sing, the better it sounds.

Attitude towards the war

What kept the *Landser* fighting even after the war was

clearly lost? A combination of three things: his culture (which almost made a fetish of honor and loyalty—practically to the point of self–destruction), blind faith, and optimism. Perhaps we could also add to this a dash of fear from his own military justice system. Even though many soldiers no longer believed in total victory, especially after the Normandy invasion, he did hope for some type of favorable political settlement; therefore he saw himself as fighting for time. The war itself was accepted as a part of life itself, and as long as the various systems were operating, the people (and soldiers) developed an *„alles klappt“* (everything is ticking over) attitude, no matter what was looming on the horizon.

Love of nature

We read again and again about how the Germans are great fans of nature and animals. The examples are legion; Albert Krupp, the great industrialist, used to have a hose leading from his lofty office above his bustling factory down to a pile of manure. To relax and give himself pleasant thoughts, he would take a big whiff through the hose. After the war, Germans who could barely get enough for themselves to eat, were seen feeding portions of their rationed bread to the geese on the lakes near Berlin. Even today, dogs are allowed in hotels and restaurants. There are many stories of Germans who carried a loyalty to their sick pets to almost ridiculous (by American standards, anyway) extremes. One of the authors of this article played host to four young German men one summer, one of whom was a member of the Border Guard. He had great expectations of conversations about history and military topics, but to his disappointment, the Border Guard turned out to be mostly interested in rocks and soccer. Two of the others were tree buffs and the fourth only wanted to take pictures of deer and woodchucks.

Class Consciousness

By American standards, this is not such an admirable custom, but one which was very much in existence during WWII Germany. The Germans call this *Stände,* and it is almost as ingrained in German culture as it is in the British. The prosperous female who rated to be addressed *„Dame"* (Lady) or *„Gnadige Frau"* (gracious lady), would boil over at the ill–mannered brute who had the audacity to call her merely *„Frau"* (Ma'am).

Despite all the "one class" posturing by the Nazis, there was some deep–seated resentment at how the *Wehrmacht* accepted non–gentry officers into its ranks. Officers from the blue–collar strata were sometimes given the derogatory name of *„VOMAG"—Volksoffizier mit Arbeiter Gesicht"* (*Volks*–officer with the face of a laborer).

Politeness

Germans seem to have this in common with most other Europeans, at least when compared with Americans. German society was (and is) very formal compared to that in America. The German language has many polite mechanisms built into it, for example the use of the informal „Du" (you) versus the formal „Sie" (you). The first is used only with very close friends (usually only one or two people qualify as "close"), children, family, and when speaking to animals. Soldiers, students and young people address each other as *„Du."* Officers on the other hand, are always addressed with the *„Sie,"* while they addressed soldiers with the informal *„Du."* (This was not true of the *Waffen–ϟϟ*) Last names were used almost exclusively among soldiers; the first name was used only in addressing one's closest *Kamerad.* Germans also placed great importance on introductions and greetings; American observers have commented on what they consider the tiring custom of shaking everyone's hand both upon entering and leaving a room.

Smoking

Smoking was such a part of life during the '40s that it cannot be emphasized enough! Items smoked and the implements to smoke with must be both accurate to the period and appropriate for a frontline soldier. Unlike today, smoking was very common during WWII.

Filterless *Zigaretten* (cigarettes) and cigars were common, as were hand–rolled cigarettes. NO FILTERED cigarettes! If you must smoke, take off the filter. Better yet, buy some European, non–filtered cigarettes such as Players. Some kind of Turkish cigarettes (quite popular then) would also be appropriate, or you might try some of the nasty French cigarettes called Galousies (not really recommended). WWII cigarettes came in paper packs or small cardboard boxes (Turkish cigarettes like these are still available at most tobacco shops).

Anzünder o. Feuerzeug (lighters) of the period came in many different styles, but the most common one looked like a chapstick container with a screw–off lid. Non–period lighters look horrible; if you need to "make fire" but don't have an authentic lighter, take some wooden matches with you.

When eating, Europeans often hold their forks upside down in their left hand. A knife, or spoon is held in the right hand. A piece of bread is held with the left hand; you break it with the right and also feed it into your mouth with the right hand. Both hands should be on the table at all times. Germans do not allow an unused hand to dangle limply at their sides.

Deutscheschaferhunde an Bett

Fahrzeug, Schwerwaffen, und Panzerwagen

Vehicles, Heavy Weapons, and Armor

Above, Feldgendarmerie on bicycles.

A single cylinder BMW.

A *Zundapp KS600* with sidecar.

A Ford truck with *Waffen SS* markings advances with motorcycle.

The interior of a Ford truck. The extra equipment makes it look the part.

A light truck of *LSSAH.*

A *Kubelwagen* transports the command group.

A rear view of a *2. Pzr. Schwimmwagen.*

2. Pzr. fieldkitchen prepares a meal.

A 2. *Pzr 7.5 cm Pak 40* or 75mm antitank gun.

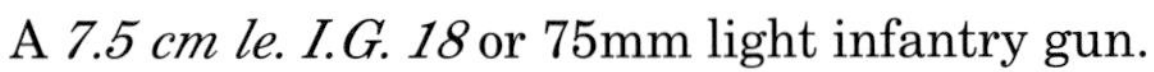

A *7.5 cm le. I.G. 18* or 75mm light infantry gun.

A *Pz. Lehr 3.7 cm Pak* or 37mm antitank gun.

Der alte Hase

Geländedienst
Land Navigation
By Erich Toby and Marsh Wise

Basic German names for landmarks

A map is called a *Karte.*

A compass is called a *Kompass,* and the directions are called *Norden (Nord), Osten (Ost), Westen (West), Süden (Süd).* Oftentimes direction is called in *Grad* (degrees). 0 degrees is north, 90 degrees east, 180 is south, etc. In the case of indirect–fire weapons, a finer unit of measure was developed called *Neugrad* (mils) which was measured in *Strich*. 360 degrees equals 6400 *Strich*. Although the small bakelite–cased march–compass is a fairly common item, the same compass with a white "A" stenciled on the cover indicates that that compass is graduated in mils rather than degrees. This is the compass for heavy weapons fire direction.

Ansprechen des Zieles, Entfernungschätzen (Identification of a target, ranging)

Objects in the foreground are in the *Vordergrund*, and the background is the *Hintergrund*.

To indicate a position either to the left or right of a visual reference point, you can use your thumb to give a relative distance to another person. A *Daumenbreite Links oder rechts* is one thumb's width left or right of a certain point when viewed over your thumb held at arm's length. A greater distance can be measured with a *Daumensprung*; if you are given a point, for example which is a *Daumensprung rechts* of a certain tree, hold your thumb out at arm's length with your right eye open and line up the tree on the right side of your thumb. Now close your right eye and open your left eye. The indicated point is on the right side of your thumb.

The situation is called the *Lage*.

The enemy is called the *Feind*.

The frontline is called the Front.

A pair of binoculars is called a *Fernglas*, or a *Doppelfernrohr*.

Range is called *Entfernung* and is measured in meters.

German	Phonetic	English
Gebaude	geh-**boy**-deh	building
Weg	vek	path
Strasse	**strah**-seh	main road
Dorf	dorf	village
Graben	**grah**-ben	ditch
Bach	bahk	creek
Fluss	flooss	river
Brucke	**bryu**-keh	bridge
See	zay	lake
Sumpt	zoomp	swamp
Waldstuck	**vald**-shtook	woodlot
Wald	valt	woods
Baum	baum	tree
Nadelbaum	**nah**-dell-baum	evergreen
Laubbaum	**lowb**-baum	deciduous tree
Baureihe	**baum**-rye-eh	line of trees
Busch	boosh	bush
Buschgruppe	**boosh**-groop-eh	patch of bushes
Baumgruppe	**bown**-groope-eh	group of trees
Waldrand	**valt**-rand	edge of woods
Waldecke	**valt**-eck-eh	corner of woods
Dorfrand	**dorf**-rand	end of village
Gabel	**gah**-bell	road fork
Feld	felt	field
Stein	shtyn	stone
Mulde	**mool**-deh	depression
Hohe	**hoe**-eh	height, hill

The enemy moves are planned and acted upon.

Above, armor advances up a road in the Ardennes.
Below, a moment in time

Deutsches Helferin

Female Impressions

Two *Nachrichten-helferine des Heeres* or Army signal auxiliaries.

Women have only begun to explore the possibilities of German reenacting. At the time of this writing women have opened several of the *Helferine* or Auxiliary areas to include nurse, signals, riding school, and flak. As World War II reenacting becomes more mainstream, it will become more like Civil War reenacting is today—more inclusive and family oriented. *SOLDAT* salutes those who are striving to make inroads for women and youth in historically accurate venues.

A *Reitlehrerin* or riding instructor.

Below, a Soviet sniper is escorted to the rear.

A front line field nurse applies bandages in battle scenario. Female auxiliaries had field uniforms as shown in historical photos of the Norwegian nursing volunteers. A first–hand account from ϟϟ *Kampfgruppe Peiper* by James Lucas adds more credence to this concept:

> *Peiper looked at the bundled shape in the uniform that stood before him. There was nothing to show that this was a woman, not until she flung back her parka hood to show the coiled plaits at either ear. "Sister Gertrude." Peiper bowed over the outstretched hand.*

Michele Milunas

Deutsches Rotes Kreuz Helferin
By Erin Warfield

The *Deutsches Rotes Kreuz Helferin* or German Red Cross nurse was a vital part of the war effort in World War II. Due to the German ideal of the three Ks—Kirche, Kindern, und Kuche (church, children, and kitchen)—women in the armed forces were unthinkable. With its entire population mobilizing for war, Germany had to enlist all the help it could get on the home front. This meant that everyone was put into some branch of service to benefit the war effort, women included. There were a few choices for women in the Third Reich if they weren't mothers, which exempted them from service. They were able to become farm workers and laborers, nurses, or one of a few other positions vital to the Reich, such as *Signalhilferin* or signal helper, and administrator for the armed forces. Nursing was often seen as the most glamorous option, so it attracted many women. To keep women out of harm's reach, field hospitals that employed female nurses were required to be at least 15 kilometers from the front lines. Wounded soldiers knew they would be all right when they found themselves in a field hospital surrounded by nurses. As one combat veteran told me, "I was wounded five times, and the pretty nurses made me heal much faster!" It was not unheard of for these field hospitals to be overrun in a fast–moving advance, so nurses were sometimes taken as prisoners, although they were generally treated with a great deal of respect for their position by the Allies.

The impression discussed here is that of the *Deutsches Rotes Kreuz Helferin* or helper nurse. These women assisted nurses by doing such things as cleaning up, feeding the wounded and assisting in minor ways in the operating room. They were also morale boosters. They would do things to help the soldier recover mentally by keeping them company, as well as meeting them at train stations and running the equivalent of the American Red Cross canteen. To reenact the German *Helferin,* the minimum necessary equipment is as follows:

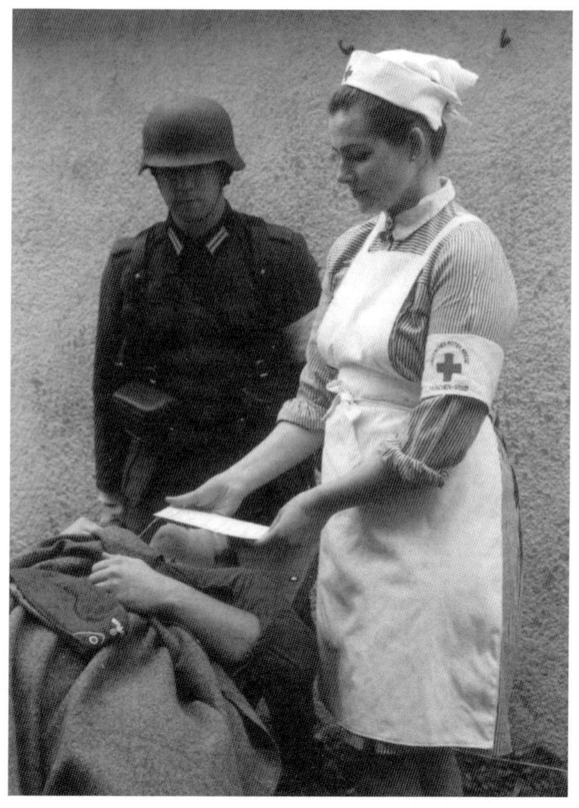

Dress: a blue and white striped dress—ending anywhere from the knees to the ankles, depending on what material shortages there were at the time—was the main uniform piece worn. The dress had narrow stripes, _ centimeter in width, running vertically up the dress with a button–on white collar (see photos). Numerous manufacturers made these dresses, so the design differentiated, but they were one–piece with buttons up the front above the waist. Some had waist ties, such as the example in the photo; others were cinched by the apron. The easiest way to get a reproduction dress is to find a seamstress in your area and have her make it up to fit you. You may be able to find simple, one piece, dress patterns at a sewing shop that will be close. You may also be able to find accurate fabric at a warehouse, although it may take a while to make. The photographed example is a late–war or postwar dress.

Collar: a separate, white, collar piece was buttoned into the dress for wear (see photo). If you have a seamstress make your dress, she should also be able to make the collar for you.

Cap: a white cap with a silk–screened or otherwise painted red cross on the front center was worn to keep the hair up and back. Ties were used to cinch it around the hair while bobby pins were used to keep it in place. This should also be reproducible by your seamstress.

Brooch: a *Deutsches Rotes Kreuz* brooch was worn at the throat of the dress. Different ranks had slightly different pins. Two examples are shown in the photographs. These can be found through militaria shows and dealers as well, as on e-bay.

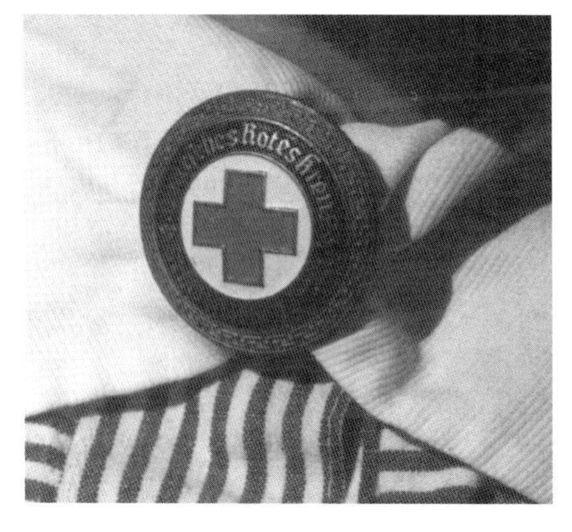

Apron: a white apron was worn over the dress. This apron had a narrow top piece and a wider bottom piece with a hidden pocket on the right–hand side. It had long ties that went over the shoulders, criss–crossed over the back, slid through loops on the sides of the dress, and came back around the front to tie. Again, your seamstress should be able to make this item.

Armband: a German Red Cross armband was worn on the upper left arm.

There were many different variations of this armband, including one with just a red cross, one with the words *Deutsches Rotes Kreuz* in Germanic font, and one in a simple font with the name of the city at the bottom.

Sleeve Triangle: a black sleeve triangle with white stitching was worn on the upper right shoulder. These triangles depicted an eagle holding a swastika in its talons and had the name of the field hospital along the bottom

Shoes: women purchased their shoes privately, so anything clunky and black will do. If you can find shoes that look like men's oxfords with a slight heel, those are ideal, but men's oxfords without a heel work as well. Both heeled and flat shoes were worn by nurses. For an added touch of authenticity, lace your shoes in the European ladder style as shown in the picture.

Stockings: if you could find them, nude, tan or brown, seamed stockings were in fashion in Germany throughout WWII. If you do choose to wear seemed stockings, they can be purchased either as pantyhose or thigh–highs through Fredericks of Hollywood.

Reference material can be found through a number of sources. As in most things to do with reenacting, I have found that interviews and conversations with veterans are the most valuable. Usually, if a German veteran is willing to talk about his experiences in the war, his time in hospitals that would have had women on staff is one of his favorite topics. Some books that have proven valuable to me for reference are *In the Service of the Reich* by John Angolia, *The German Army Medical Corps in World War II* by Alex Buchner and *German Uniforms of the Third Reich 1933-1945* by Brian L. Davis. For first –person accounts by German nurses, I would recommend *Berlin Diaries* by Marie Vassiltchikov, a white Russian princess living in Berlin throughout the war. She became a nurse at the end of the war and recalls her time in the hospital. I would also recommend *Under Hitler's Banner* by Edmund Blandford, a collection of recollections from men and women in many branches of service in Germany during World War II. This is also a good read if you are interested in what was happening, from the German perspective, throughout the war, both in the country and on the front. One other book that has been worthwhile is *The World Within War* by Gerald Linderman. It gives accounts of medics in the chapter entitled "Fighting the Germans: The War of Rules as well as the 'rules and regulations'" governing medical personnel and how these rules were upheld and broken. All of these books are currently in print and can be purchased by special order from most chain bookstores.

Reenacting the German nurse opens up many interesting conversations with visitors at public displays, giving you the opportunity to explain a wide variety of topics such as women's roles in the war (Germany was the only country that never officially enlisted women), the Geneva Convention and the meaning of the Red Cross. My greatest moment while reenacting the German nurse was when I was at a public battle. I came out after the site was open to the public, and as I walked up the path, I had a German veteran come running up to me saying, "Yes! That's exactly what the nurses looked like! I was wounded five times and the pretty nurses made me heal much faster!"

Just behind the front line is the divisional *Kranken Sammelstelle* where today a well known actress and singer Gerda Kino is visiting the wounded and the staff of the heroic *Großdeutschland Panzer Division.*

Film Star to the Front with *Großdeutschland*
By Karl Lehmann *KB Zug*

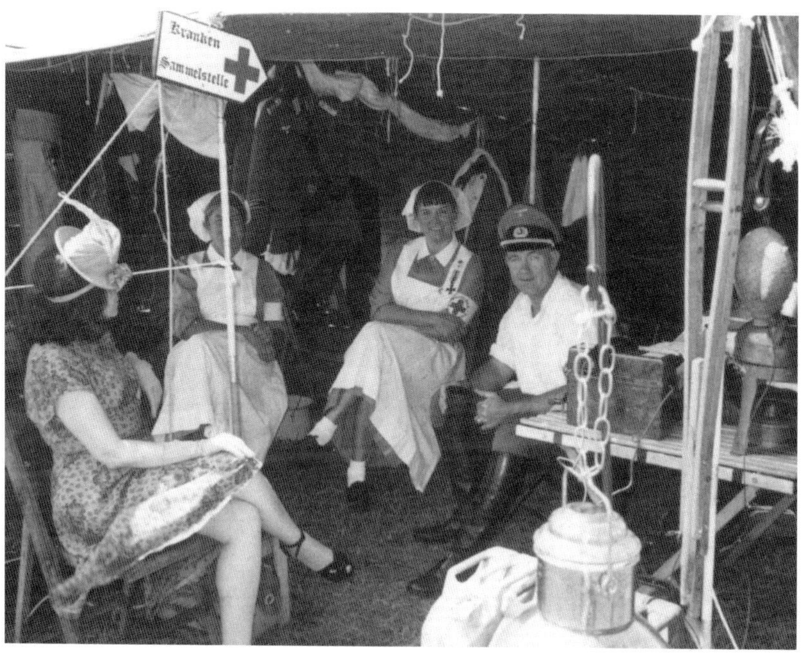

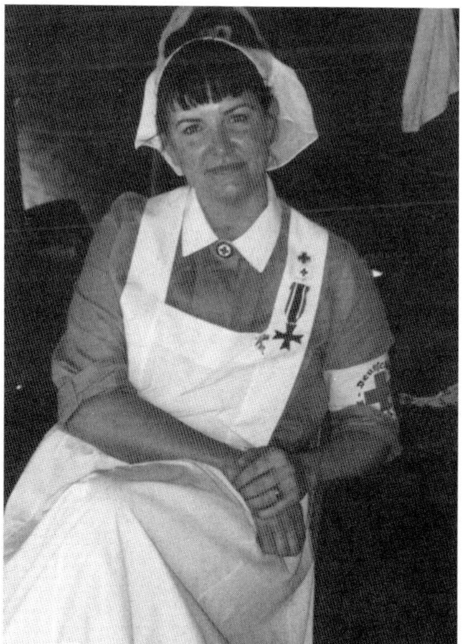

Above, before visiting the wounded and ill, Gerda takes a moment with two *Kranken-schwester* and the *Stabartz.*

For her contribution to the care of the sick and wounded, this *Krankenschwester* has been awarded with the *Kriegsverdienstkreuz II Klasse.*

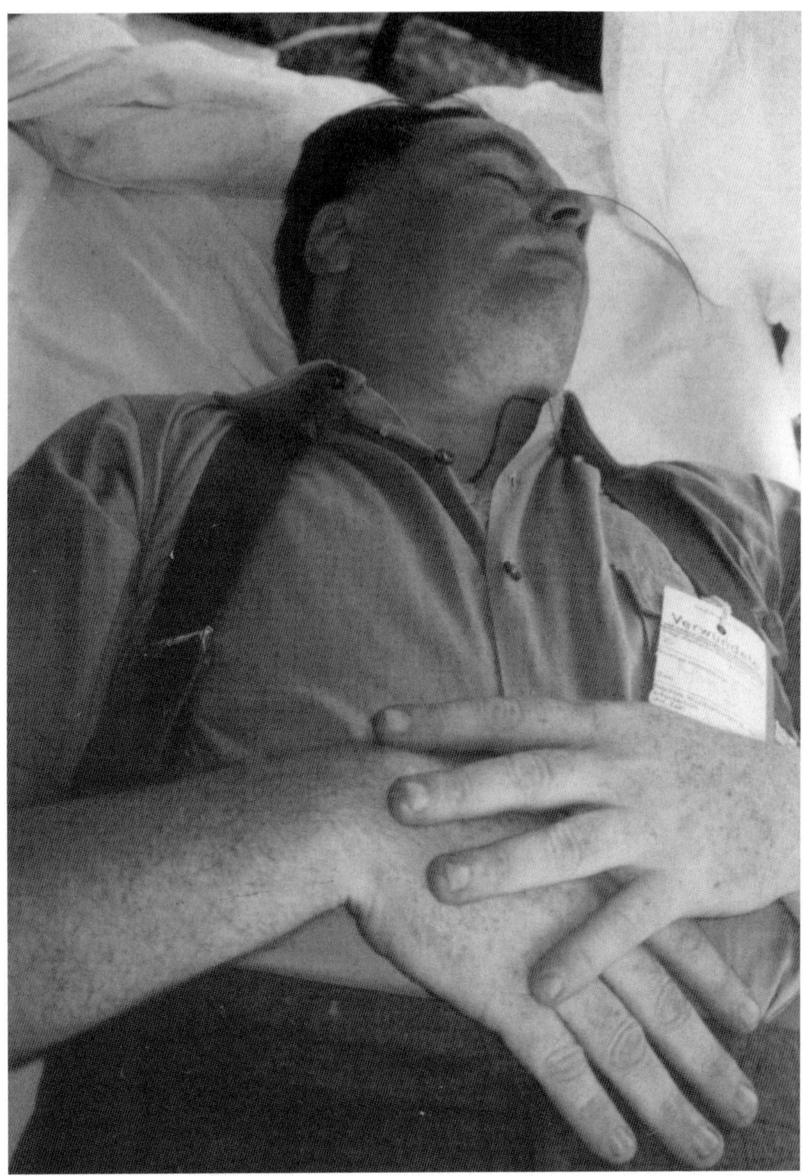

Now resting quietly, this *Großdeutschen* slumbers through the visit. Not wishing to wake him, Gerda stoops to place a gentle kiss on the cheek and a whispered *"Vielen Dank, Soldat!"* in the ear. Was it a dream?

Honoring Those We Remember

Ceremonial wreaths remember those of *Großdeutschland.*

One of the prime underlying reasons given to the "Why do you do this?" question is that it honors and remembers the men and women who were the history makers in the great conflict of 1939–1945. For those reenacting GI, there are numerous ways to accomplish this with relative ease. However, for those who have chosen the German impression the task is much more difficult.

As with all the other difficulties to be overcome, this too falls to a group with vision and drive. In this case that is *Großdeutschland.* Traveling to Germany, a unit contingent attended the annual *Großdeutschland* Veterans' Reunion. The old and the young *Großdeutschen* shared unique moments that can only be dreamed about by those who have not made this giant step.

The Honor Guard at the memorial ceremony. Here the visiting Americans were recognized.

Großdeutschland unit commander Robert Lawrence presents a truly American gift—the flag of the United States of America.

General Safety Regulations for German Combat Units

Due to the unique nature of our hobby, it should be obvious that there is always the potential for a unit member to be injured at an event. Keeping this in mind, units should established a comprehensive list of policies to minimize the possibility of injury and protect participants while in the field or in garrison.

It is the responsibility of each unit member to prohibit other participants from committing unsafe acts. If the individual committing the unsafe act continues, the violation must be reported to preclude injury to other innocent participants.

Overall Organizational Examples (HRS)

- All sponsoring groups (chapters, units, etc.) are required to appoint a safety officer to represent EACH side at any event where blank ammunition and/or pyrotechnics are used. These officers must be registered with the Chairman of the Safety Committee at least 30 days prior to the event. These may be permanent appointments at the Chairman's discretion.
- All participants must be a member of a recognized unit or a unit–forming. Note that if a unit–forming has fewer than five members present at said event, they must attach themselves to another group willing to vouch for their safe conduct.
- All commanders must be at least 21 years of age and agree to be responsible for the safety and authenticity of ALL participants serving as a member of his unit. "Freelancing" (serving without proper unit affiliation) is grounds for dismissal from an event.

- All motor vehicles participating in an event must be driven by a licensed driver in a sensible manner.
- Any vehicle being driven off–road must be preceded by a ground guide to avoid personnel hiding in sur rounding foliage.
- Absolutely NO ignitable devices are to be thrown or projected at or near any motor vehicle.
- All battles involving possession of one or more buildings (Bunker Battles) must be under the control of one or more neutral observers with the authority to stop all activity. Appointment may be made on site.
- No alcoholic beverages are to be consumed at the event in violation of local ordinance.
- No weapon is to be discharged directly at a person at less than 20 yards.
- All pyrotechnics must be approved by the event's safety officers.
- No horizontally fired projectiles (fired at a trajectory of less than 45°) are permitted.
- All vertically fired projectiles must have approved frangible warheads and not weigh over 12 ounces.
- No live ammunition is to be brought to an event. Violation of this rule will result in dismissal of the offender from the HRS
- Wood–tipped blanks may only be used by automatic weapons equipped with a shredder.
- Affixed bayonets are expressly forbidden. Shotguns may be licensed by the HRS and are subject to such rules as stated with their licenses.
- The use of metal–bodied parachute flares, artillery simulators, or other high explosive simulators are forbidden at all events. Devices of this type may be used at staged, spectator events under the total su pervision of a safety officer, provided the devices

are detonated only in a controlled area.

- Refusal to obey the decision of the safety officers will result in a report filed with the Chairman of Safety Committee who will submit a request to the Board of Directors for the dismissal of the offender from the HRS within thirty (30) days.

Additional Unit Level Safety Regulations

- HRS safety regulations must be followed.
- At each event, the unit will conduct a safety inspection of all members during formation prior to movement to the field. Leaders will inspect their men for live ammunition and dangerous pyrotechnics. All ammo pouches, magazines, grenade bags and weapons will be checked.
- Unit members may be subject to a safety inspection by an Event Sponsor–appointed safety officer.
- No weapon will be loaded prior to movement to the field. Once at the field site, the command will be given to load weapons. Even at the field site, weapons should be placed on "Safe" and rounds unchambered when not actually participating in action against enemy forces.
- Weapons will not be loaded when embarking or disembarking from any mode of transportation.

General Field Safety

- If umpires are utilized in the field, all unit members will abide by the umpire rulings.
- To prevent concussion injury, weapons will not be discharged above or behind the heads of personnel in positions to the firer's front.
- If a person is injured during a battle, stop the action until the injured person is tended to or removed from the battle area.

- Personnel with medical conditions should alert the senior unit member in attendance. These personnel should also wear a medical identification tag to alert medical personnel while being treated.
- Do not drink water from local streams, rivers, ponds, or lakes.
- If a grass fire occurs, immediately stop the battle and extinguish the flames. In some geographic area, fires will spread out of control very quickly.

Camp Safety

- Camp fires will not be started unless approved by the property owner. Fires will be limited to approved areas and will not be left unattended. All fires must be COMPLETELY extinguished.
- Keep lanterns, stoves and candles away from tentage and other flammable materials/substances.
- All vehicles moved at the camp site will have ground guides.
- Use of alcohol is discouraged and at some events is prohibited.
- Use of drugs (other than prescription) by any unit member at any event is STRICTLY PROHIBITED.

Hot Weather Safety

- Wear light clothing such as HBT uniforms when ambient temperatures are high. Unit leaders must be aware of these dangers and direct uniform modifications.
- Drink a canteen of water before moving out; take a full canteen to the field and drink it. Extra water can be loaded in vehicles.
- Rest frequently as necessary. Loosen restrictive clothing and equipment.

- During warm weather events, carry only the equipment necessary.
- Leaders learn to recognize heat injury indicators and watch your *Soldaten!*

Cold Weather Safety

- Layer clothing, remove or add as necessary.
- Bring extra socks, uniforms and gloves in the event the first uniform becomes wet.
- Bring a scarf or toque to protect the face and ears.
- Waterproof footwear and change wet socks.
- Use period felt–leather boots along with padded winter over–uniforms in dry cold.
- Drink water to replace fluids lost through perspiration.
- Leaders learn to recognize cold weather injury indicators and watch your *Soldaten!*

Großdeutschen und Windhund. Reporting to the commander, another enemy drive has been thwarted!

Der alte Hase

AWARDS AND DECORATIONS
L⚡⚡AH Proven Method

This section is provided to help units establish a method for the award and wear of Awards and Decorations. This is a system designed and used by L⚡⚡AH, the largest and one of the oldest German units. While units may choose to take a different path, this system provides unit members with tangible evidence in recognition of participation, exceptional leadership, service or achievement, and military service while maintaining a system which realistically duplicates that used by the World War II German military.

From this point I have not edited the work of L⚡⚡AH. Interject your own unit characteristics as they work best.

CRITERIA FOR INDIVIDUAL AWARDS AND DECORATIONS

Individual awards and decorations are earned and awarded based on an ACT/ECP (Actual Combat Time/ Earned Credit Points) system. This system authorizes awards for active participation and attendance at authorized events or functions. For purposes of clarity, the following information is provided:

A. Event/Battle – Any L⚡⚡AH–approved tactical or non–tactical gathering of ten (10) or more unit members for the purpose of furthering the objectives of the LAH. Exception to the ten–member rule may be authorized by the Regimental Commander.
B. Actual Combat time (ACT) –Time actually spent in uniform while conducting tactical maneuvers against an armed opponent. Time spent in the con-

duct of guard duty or other official functions may also be counted towards ACT credit at the discretion of the *Batallionführer*. One hour equals one ACT. Cumulative ACTs may also be counted towards ECPs for purposes of event credit. Personnel participating in authentic camping will be authorized an additional 5 ACTs for each night camped in the field or at an approved campsite.

C. Earned Credit Points (ECP) – One ECP will be awarded for each twenty–five (25) miles spent traveling, one way, to an authorized event up to 500 miles. Travel over 500 miles will count as double points. Example: a member travels 1,000 miles (one way) to an event. The first 500 miles are equal to twenty (20) ECPs. The
second 500 miles are equal to an additional forty (40) ECPs for a cumulative total of sixty (60) ECPs. Members attending events from overseas locations will be awarded ECPs in accordance with *Regimentführer* Directives.
    1. One ECP will be awarded for each day actually participating in an event.
    2. One ECP will be awarded for every four (4) ACTs at an event.
    3. Special ECP and/or ACT point values may be authorized at the discretion of the *Batallionführer* or designated representative.

D. Leadership – Defined as demonstrated performance of duty so exceptional and well above that of his peers that it has directly resulted in significantly improving the tactical impression or proficiency or administrative performance of his section or of the unit. An example would be the development and implementation of a training program which improves the unit's ability to such a degree that it results in the achievement of numerous victories in the field. Demonstrated supervision and control of subordinates are two key areas which will be evaluated for award of any leadership decorations.

E. Service – Defined as service or contributions which, over a sustained period of time, clearly distinguish the member from his peers. Examples would be publishing a series of useful newsletter articles on reenacting (not after–action reports), providing the unit with a reputable source of inexpensive equipment or uniforms, etc.

F. Achievement – Defined as an act or series of acts well above the expected performance of duty or a contribution so unique or exceptional that it has an impact which very significantly affects the member's unit or reenacting as a whole. It may increase morale, enhance authenticity, or improve performance or proficiency (not related to leadership). Examples would be the recruitment of several new quality members, purchase or construction and utilization of a WWII vehicle, etc.

G. Military Service – Recognition of unit members who have honorably served or are presently serving in the US Armed Forces in any component, Active, Reserve or National Guard.

MEDALS, BADGES, RIBBON BARS, AND AWARD CRITERIA

A. Awards Authorized for Individual Participation
   1. Cuff Title "Adolf Hitler" (*Armelband "Adolf Hitler"*) – Awarded to Kandidats upon successful completion of three (3) officially recognized events as a paid LAH member.
   2. Infantry Assault Badge

(*Infanterie Sturmabzeichen*) – Awarded in two classes:

(a) Bronze (*Bronz*) – For accumulation of 50 ACTs for members who have no prior military service in the US Armed Forces.

(b) Silver (Silber) – For accumulation of 50 ACTs for members who have served military duty in one of the US Armed Forces.

3. Iron Cross 2nd Class (*Eisernes Kreuz II. Klasse*) – For accumulation of 85 ACTs.
4. Iron Cross 1st Class (Eisernes Kreuz I. Klasse) – For accumulation of 125 ACTs and must have been awarded the Iron Cross 2nd Class.
5. Close Combat Clasp (Nahkampfspange) – Awarded in three classes:
   (a) Bronze (*Bronz*) – For accumulation of 175 ACTs.
   (b) Silver (*Silber*) – For accumulation of 250 ACTs.
   (c) Gold (*Gold*) – For accumulation of 450 ACTs.
6. Wound Badge 1939 (*Werwundetenabzeichen*) – Awarded in three classes:
   (a) Black (*Schwarz*) – For sustaining an injury incurred while actually engaged in tactical maneuvers requiring a licensed physician's attention. Documentation required. Also awarded for attending a cumulative total of 25 events without sustaining an injury.
   (b) Silver (*Silber*) – For accumulation of two injuries incurred while actually engaged in tactical maneuvers requiring a licensed physician's attention. Docu-

mentation required. Also awarded for attending a cumulative total of 50 events without sustaining an injury.

(c) Gold (*Gold*) – For accumulation of three injuries incurred while actually engaged in tactical maneuvers requiring a licensed physician's attention. Documentation required. Also awarded for attending a cumulative total of 75 events without sustaining an injury. The class of Wound Badge awarded may also be determined by the severity of the injury incurred. This determination will be made by the Bataillon Stab on a case–by–case basis.

7. Tank Assault Badge (Panzerkampfabzeichen) – Awarded in two classes:
   (a) Bronze (*Bronz*) – For participation at five (5) events as an actual crewmember (not passenger) of an original or approved reproduction armored vehicle.
   (b) Silver (*Silber*) – For participation at fifteen (15) events as an actual crewmember (not passenger) of an original or approved reproduction armored vehicle.
8. East Medal (*Ostmedaille*) – Awarded for participation in five (5) Russian Front events.
9. Kuban Shield (*Kuban–Schild*) – Awarded to en listed men and NCOs for participation in a total of ten (10) Russian Front events.
10. Crimea Shield (*Krim–Schild*) – Awarded to officers for participation in a total of ten (10) Russian Front events.
11. Anti–Partisan War Badge (Bandenkampfabzeichen) – Awarded in three classes:
    (a) Bronze (*Bronz*) – Awarded for partici-

pation in fifteen (15) Russian Front events.

(b) Silver (*Silber*) – Awarded for participation in twenty (20) Russian Front events.

(c) Gold (*Gold*) – Awarded for participation in twenty–five (25) Russian Front events.

12. Driver's Badge of Merit (Kraftfahr–Bewahrungsabzeichen) – Awarded in three classes:

(a) Bronze (*Bronz*) – Awarded for participation at five (5) events as an authorized and designated driver of an original or approved reproduction wheeled vehicle.

(b) Silver (Silber) – Awarded for participation at ten (10) events as an authorized and designated driver of an original or approved reproduction wheeled vehicle.

(c) Gold (*Gold*) – Awarded for participation at twenty (20) events as an authorized and designated driver of an original or approved reproduction wheeled vehicle.

13. Special Badge for Single–Handed Tank Destruction (*Sonderabzeichen für das Niederkampfen von Panzerkampfenwagen durch Einzelkampfer*) – Awarded for the single–handed destruction or capture of an Allied tank while avoiding capture or "death." One badge may also be awarded for every three (3) armored vehicles destroyed in the absence of tanks. It must be emphasized that qualification for this award is based upon single–handed destruction, not while serving as a member of a crew served weapon. Documentation must be submitted and verified by two LAH witnesses.

(a) Silver (*Silber*) – One silver badge for each tank destroyed (or one badge for each three armored vehicles destroyed) up to four badges.

(b) Gold (*Gold*) – One gold badge for each five tanks destroyed (or one gold badge for 15 armored vehicles destroyed). Once the gold badge is awarded, the four silver badges must be removed.

AWARDS AUTHORIZED FOR ADVANCED PARTICIPATION

This category of awards recognizes unit members for advanced participation (ECPs in excess of 600 points). Two categories have been established in order to allow Category A members (up to age 39) wear Third Reich era awards and to allow Category B veterans (age 40 and above) wear World War I period awards.

A. 600 ECPs
   1. Czech/Sudetenland Annexation Medal (*Medaille zur Erinnerung an der 1. Oktober 1938*)
   2. Silesian Eagle (*Schlesischer Adler*)

B. 800 ECPs
   1. Defense Wall Honor Award–West Wall (*Deutsches Schutzwall–Ehrenzeichen*)
   2. Baltic Cross (*Baltisches Kreuz*)

C. 1,000 ECPs
   1. Prague Castle Bar (*Spange "Prager Burg"*)
   2. Bavarian Military Max Joseph Order (*Bayern Militar Max–Joseph Orden*)

D. 1,400 ECPs
   1. Austrian Annexation Medal of 1938 (*Medaille zur Erinnerung an der 13. Marz 1938*)
   2. Bavarian Military Service Order (*Bayern Militar Verdienst Orden)*

AWARDS AUTHORIZED FOR LAH MEMBERSHIP

A. Old Campaigner's Chevron (*Ehrenwinkel für Alte Kampfer*) – Awarded to SS–Unterscharführers and above for ten (10) years continuous membership as a member of the LAH.

B. SS Long Service Award (SS–Dienstauszeichenungen) Awarded in four classes:
   1. Fourth Class – Awarded for three (3) years membership in the LAH.
   2. Third Class – Awarded for five (5) years membership in the LAH.
   3. Second Class – Awarded for eight (8) years membership in the LAH.
   4. First Class – Awarded for twelve (12) years membership in the LAH.

AWARDS AUTHORIZED FOR EXCEPTIONAL LEADERSHIP, SERVICE OR ACHIEVEMENT

A. Knight's Cross to the Iron Cross (Ritterkreuz des Eisernes Kreuz)
   1. Knight's Cross (*Ritterkreuz*)
   2. Knight's Cross with Oakleaves (*mit Eichenlaub*)
   3. Knight's Cross with Oakleaves and Swords (*mit Eichenlaub und Schwerten*)

B. Knight's Cross to the War Service Cross (*Ritterkreuz des Kriegsverdienstkreuz*) with or without Swords

C. War Order of the German Cross in Gold (*Kriegs Order des Deutches Kreuzes in Gold*)

D. War Service Cross (*Kriegsverdienst Kreuz*) – Awarded in two classes:
   1. First Class, with or without Swords
   2. Second Class, with or without Swords

E. Decoration of 9 November 1923–Blood Order

(*Ehrenzeichen von 9. November 1923- Blutorden*) – Awarded for accomplishments above unit level.

F. Honor Roll Clasp of the German Army (*Ehrenblatt-Spange des Heeres*) – Awarded by the Regimental Commander only. Recipient must hold the Iron Cross 1st and 2nd Class.

AUTHORIZED AWARDS FOR MILITARY SERVICE (Equivalency Awards)

US Military Award qualifies for	**German Award**
Congressional Medal of Honor	Knight's Cross
Distinguished Service Cross	War Order of the German Cross
Distinguished Service Medal	Silver Star
Legion of Merit	Distinguished Flying Cross
Bronze Star	Soldier's Medal
Purple Heart	Wound Badge in Gold
Meritorious Service Medal	Iron Cross 1st Class
Air Medal	Joint Service Commendation Medal
Army Commendation Medal	Iron Cross 2nd Class
National Defense Service Medal	Army Achievement Medal
Good Conduct Medal	Combat Infantry Badge
Close Combat	Clasp in Gold
Vietnam Service Medal	War Merit Cross with Swords
Southwest Asia Service Medal (Expert Infantry Badge)	Infantry Assault Badge in Silver
Parachutist Badge	*Luftwaffe* Parachutist Badge
Aviator Wings	*Luftwaffe* Pilot Badge
Crewchief Wings	*Luftwaffe* Observer Badge
Aircrew Wings	*Luftwaffe* Gunners Badge (Observer)

ARMED FORCES LONG SERVICE AWARDS

Wehrmacht Long Service Awards are authorized for prior or present military service in the US Army, Air Force, Navy, Marines, Coast Guard, or Reserve/National Guard units of these branches as follows:

A. 4th Class, for four (4) years service
B. 3rd Class, for five (5) to twelve (12) years service
C. 2nd Class, for thirteen (13) to eighteen (18) years service
D. 1st Class, for nineteen (19) to twenty–five (25) years service
E. 1st Class with Oakleaves, for twenty–six (26) to forty (40) years service No more than two *Wehrmacht* Long Service ribbons will be worn at one time. Documentation (DD Form 214) required.

MISCELLANEOUS AWARDS AND AWARD CRITERIA

Additional civilian or military acquired skills may qualify for a German equivalency award. Issuance of any other awards not covered in this manual must be reviewed and approved by the *Bataillon Stab* on a case–by–case basis.

AWARD PRECEDENCE AND METHOD OF WEAR

Awards are worn on the wearer's left breast pocket with the highest award centered on the pocket. Lesser awards are worn on the bottom of the pocket with the most prestigious to the wearer's right (nearer the heart.) Pinback awards are normally worn suspended from small loops, not pushed through the uniform fabric. Close Combat Bars are worn above the left pocket above bar of awarded ribbons. Iron Cross, War Merit Cross, and Eastern Front Medal ribbons taken directly from the award can be worn without a bar inserted through the second button hole and sewn behind the tunic flap. The most prestigious is worn most exposed. The order of precedence is Iron Cross, War Merit Cross, Eastern Front Medal.

Another day ends in victory!

Der alte Hase

GERMAN BASIC MILITARY TRAINING LSSAH

1. INDIVIDUAL TRAINING

Individual training is very important in reenacting. How good the unit looks in the field depends on each and every member. Study and use of period drill and tactics will make a stand out historically, and is reflected in the spirit shown not only in combat but on the drill field. The key to a good imprssion is an eye for detail in all you do as a reenactor. You leave behind the modern world and physically step into the 1940s to look and act as a *Soldat.* To present yourself as a *Soldat,* follow these basic guide lines from the LSSAH manual:

A. Always fall in at attention.
B. If you have a weapon, fall in at order arms.
C. When called to attention, click your heels.
D. Always fall in with a soft cap unless in a tactical situation or are ordered otherwise.
E. When you speak, always state the rank and name of the person you are addressing.
F. The German hand salute is somewhat between a British full hand salute and an American flat hand salute. Rotate your right hand to a 45–degree angle and touch your right eyebrow with the hand slightly cupped. Absolutely no political salutes are to be rendered.

G. The first, and generally the last, formations of the day require service dress only and no combat gear unless otherwise ordered by the ranking man.

H. When placed at rest while in formation, remain in formation. If you must leave the formation, inform your squad leader *(Gruppenführer)* first.

If followed these items will make unit formations will be much more organized and will leave a distinct impression on observers.

2. GERMAN COMMANDS

To enable the individual to execute any military movements, the mastering of the essential German commands is necessary. The following list and description of the German commands used in the *Leibstandarte* should be studied and practiced:

A. *„ANGETRETEN!"* Fall in! Same as in the US Army. *Gruppenführer* establishes the right side of the formation and the rest fall in to his left in a straight line.

B. *„STILLGE STANDEN!"* Attention! Body rigid, heels together, and toes at a 45–degree angle of each other, hands with palms flat against upper thighs, elbows out slightly from the body, and eyes front. An example of a formation with the soldiers at *„Stillgestand*

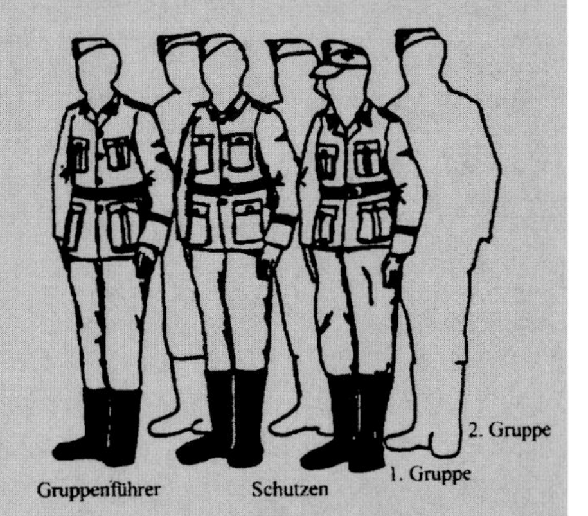

Figure 10-1

en!"The men are aligned abreast of their *Gruppenführer*, who is on the formation's right, hands down at their sides, palms flat against the upper thighs, and elbows slightly away from the body. Feet are together at the heels, and toes are at 45–degree angles. Immediately behind the *1. Gruppe* is the outline of the *2. Gruppe,* who falls in directly behind. Important: when you speak of the right or the left of formation, you are speaking as if you are standing within the formation. The officer or NCO giving commands must take this into consideration before executing movement. For example, if the NCO gives *„Recht Um!"* it would be the formation's right in which he is commanding them to turn, not toward his right.

C. *„AUFSCHIESSEN! ANGETRETEN!"* At close interval, dress right, fall in. While at attention, eyes right, and dress on the *Gruppenführer*, while at the same time the left hand is made into a fist and is placed on the left hip. The right hand remains on the upper right thigh. As soon as you are dressed to the *Gruppenführer*, return to position of attention, eyes front, and left hand on upper left thigh. *„Aufschliessen!"* is illustrated in Figure 10-2. The *Gruppenführer* is on the right of the formation with the remainder of his *Gruppe* dressing on him. Note: the men are looking to their right to align with the *Gruppenführer* and that their left hand is in a fist resting on their left hip. The left elbow is extended

Figure 10-2

to touch the right arm of the man beside them. The right hand is in normal position while at attention. The *Gruppenführer* has quickly dressed with his left elbow and resumed the position of attention. Every man in his *Gruppe* will do the same after dressing.

D. *„RUHRT EUCH!“* At Ease! At the command, the feet are moved to shoulder width apart, left foot slightly forward of the right, arms hanging down to the sides with hands relaxed and cupped. Head and eyes straight ahead.

E. *„RECHT UM!“* Right Face! The movement is the same as for the US Army. Rotate to the right by turning on the right heel while turning and pushing to the right with the ball of the left foot. After facing is completed, bring left foot in line with the right, assuming the position of attention.

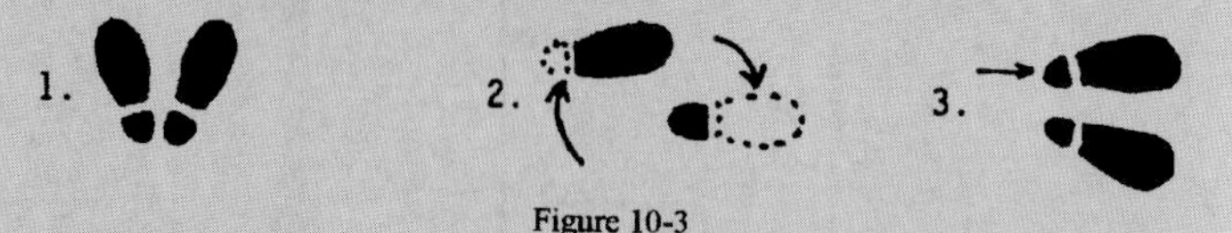

Figure 10-3

F. *„LINKS UM!“* Left Face! The movement is the same as for the US Army. Rotate to the left by turning on the left heel while turning and pushing to the left with the ball of the right foot. After the facing movement is completed, bring the right foot in line with the left, assuming the position of attention.

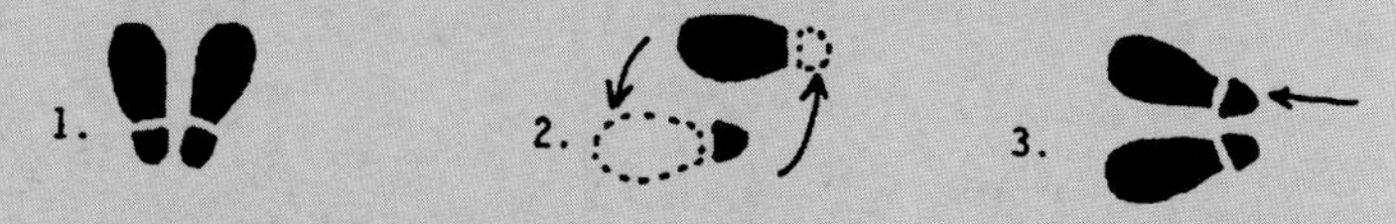

Figure 10-4

G. *„KEHRT UM!“* About Face! The Germans execute this command the opposite of the US Army. At the command, the left foot is moved to the rear with the left toe in line with the right heel. Rotate to the left on both heels, 180 degrees. The right toe should be in line with the left heel at this point. Bring the right foot in line with the left and resume the position of attention.

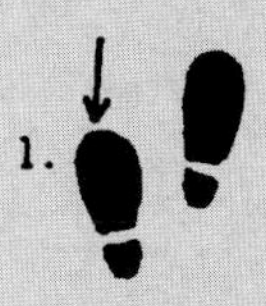

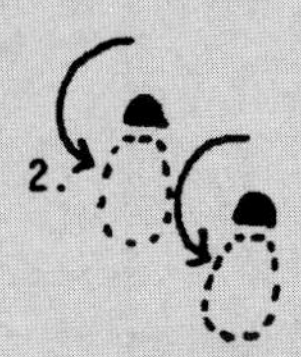

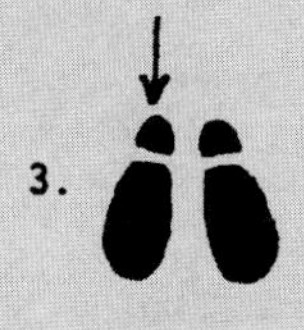

Figure 10-5

H. *WEGTRETEN!"* Fall Out! Simply execute a „Kehrt *Um!"* and walk away.

I. *„AUGEN RECHT!"* Eyes Right! At the command, the head and eyes snap to the right with out moving the body. Hold this position until ordered to "front." If you are given this command during inspection, you are expected to follow the movement of the inspecting officer until your head and eyes are facing directly front. Head and eyes remain to the front.

J. *„AUGEN LINKS!"* Eyes Left! Same as for *„Augen Recht"* except to the left.

K. *„AUGEN GERADE AUS!"* Eyes Front! The head and eyes are moved from the *„Augen Recht"* or *„Augen Links"* position to facing directly forward.

3. MARCHING COMMANDS

A. (*Kompanie, Zug, Gruppe,* etc.), *„MARSCH!"* March! This command is the same as for the US Army. At the command, the soldier steps off with the left foot, taking a full step. Hands would swing to the cadence and when either hand comes forward, it is brought across the front of the body, nearly up to the belt buckle, in a sharp motion.

B. (*Kompanie, Zug, Gruppe,* etc.), *„HALT!“* Halt! Same as for the US Army. On the foot that the command *„Halt!“* is given, take one more complete step with the other foot and bring the trailing foot in line with it and stop.

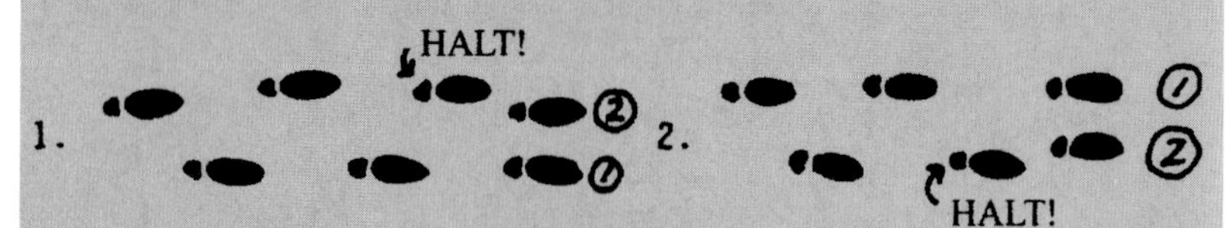

Figure 10-6

C. *„RECHTSSCHWENGT, MARSCH!“* Column Right, March! Same as for the US Army. When the column needs to be turned to the right, either while stationary or moving, the command is always given when the right foot strikes the ground. Bring the left foot up a full step and pivot to the right, 90 degrees, on the ball of the left foot. Continue to march in the new direction.

Figure 10-7

D. *„LINKSSCHWENGT, MARSCH!“* Column Left, March! Same as for the US Army. When the column needs to be turned to the left, either while stationary or moving, the command is always given when the left foot strikes the ground. Bring the right foot up a full step and pivot 90 degrees to the left on the ball of the right foot. Continue to march in the new direction.

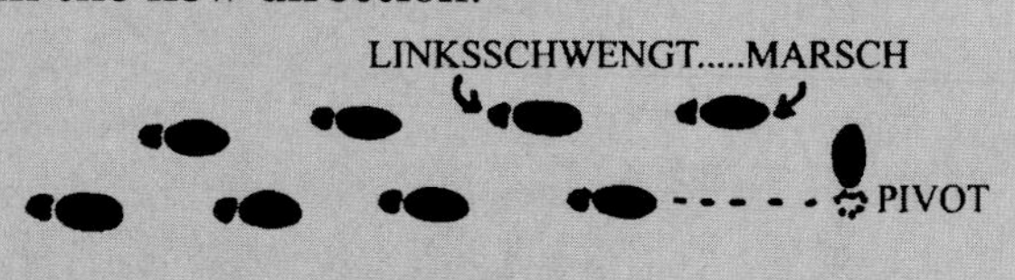

Figure 10-8

E. *„IN REIHE, MARSCH!“* In Combat Column, March! From the basic formation or while in column with two or more *Gruppen*, the unit is to form a single file line consisting of each Gruppe lined up in numerical order (i.e., 1, 2, 3, etc.). The *Gruppenführer* of the *Gruppe* leads out and when the last man of his *Gruppe* passes the *Gruppenführer* of the second *Gruppe*, that *Gruppenführer* and his *Gruppe* follow. This continues until all *Gruppen* are in column.

4. WEAPONS DRILL

A. *„DAS GEWEHR, AB!“* Order Arms! When ordered to *„Angetreten“* (Fall in), always stand at “Order Arms” and at “Attention” with heels together and toes out at 45–degree angles. The weapon is held on the right side with butt plate on the ground next to the right foot. The lower end of the butt plate should be aligned with the right toe of your boot. Right hand fingers should be extended and joined, grasping the rifle at the top barrel band with knuckles facing the front, elbow slightly out from the side. Left arm in the “Attention” position with palm of hand on upper thigh and elbow slightly out from the side.

B. *„DAS GEWEHR, UBER!“* Left Shoulder Arms! The *Waffen–ᛋᛋ* as well as the *Heer*, shouldered the rifle to the left shoulder instead of to the right unlike many other armies of the world. From the *„Ab“* (order) position, the weapon is brought directly in front of the body with the right hand level with the chin and the left hand catching the rifle just below the right. The weapon is approximately one foot from the chest and in line with the tunic buttons. The bolt of the rifle is facing to the soldier’s right and the left side of the weapon is toward the body. To move the weapon to the left shoulder, the right hand drops to the comb of the stock (the area just behind

Figure 10-9

the bolt), rotates the rifle 90 degrees counterclockwise while simultaneously moving the left hand to the butt of the stock and raising the weapon onto the left shoulder. When the weapon is correctly placed on the left shoulder, the heel of the butt is pulled in against the side of the body just below the belt of the tunic, and the left elbow is slightly out from the body. The weapon should appear nearly vertical to the body. At the moment the weapon is in place, the right hand is dropped sharply to the right side, returning to the "Attention" position.

C. *„ACHTUNG! PRASENTIERT, DAS GEWEHR!"* Attention! Present Arms! This command was only given when the soldier was at "Left Shoulder Arms." At the command *„Achtung,"* bring the right hand up to the comb of the stock with fingers extended and joined, and simultaneously rotate the butt of the weapon with the left hand 90 degrees in a clockwise motion. This will place the right side of the weapon facing away from the body and the left against the body. At the command *„Prasentiert,*

Figure 10-10

Das Gewehr, "rotate the weapon another 90 degrees clockwise with the right hand which was on the comb of the stock and at the same time release the butt of the stock with the left hand. Move the left hand up along the left side of the stock and grasp the weapon next to the lower sight. The left hand should have fingers extended and joined with knuckles facing away from the body and the thumb pointing up along the left side of the weapon. Simply straighten the extended and joined four fingers of the right hand just below the trigger guard, leaving the thumb up under the bolt next to the body. Weapon location should be directly over the left breast pocket parallel to the body with trigger guard facing away from the body. The top barrel band should be level with and centered on the left eye.

D. *„DAS GEWEHR, UBER!"* Left Shoulder Arms! After "Present Arms," the soldier is ordered to the "Left Shoulder Arms" position. It is done in near reverse order. Release the left hand and move it back down to the butt of the stock while simultaneously rotating the weapon 180 degrees, counterclockwise, with the right hand still on the comb of the stock. With the left hand on the butt of the stock and the right hand as a guide, place the weapon back on the left shoulder.

Figure 10-11

Figure 10-12

When the rifle is in place, bring the right hand sharply back to the side in the position of "Attention."

E. *„DAS GEWEHR, AB!"* Order Arms! This command is given while at *„Das Gewehr, Uber"* (Left Shoulder Arms). It enables the soldier to bring the rifle from the left shoulder and place the butt of the rifle on the ground. At the command, simultaneously drop the left arm, rotate the rifle to the right and grasp and top barrel band with the right hand. Then, release the rifle stock with the left hand and simultaneously swing the rifle to the right, with the right forearm parallel to the ground. The last movement is to place the butt of the rifle onto the ground, even with the toe of the right foot.

F. „GEWEHR, UMHANGEN!" Sling Arms! This command is only given when weapons are at *„Ab"* (order arms). At the command, the sling is loosened and the weapon is slung over the right shoulder.

Figure 10-13

The right hand should hold the sling up near the right breast pocket and the elbow should be pulled in to the side. NOTE: If marching in column—halt and left face into *Zug* formation, the weapon is automatically brought to the *„Gewehr, Ab,"* (order arms) position.

5. FORMING THE UNIT

A. *GRUPPE* or (squad) consists of a total of ten men; a *Gruppenführer* (squad leader), *Truppenführer* (assistant squad leader), a *Maschinengewehrschutz* (machine gunner), and seven *Gewehrschutz* (riflemen). The basic formation of the *Gruppe* is *„In Linie"* (squad line). An example of Gruppe *„In Linie"* formation is given in Figure 10-14. The command is given *„Gruppe, In Linie, Angetreten!,"* and the *Gruppenführer* is the first to fall in. He will fall in facing the *Zugführer*; the remainder of the *Gruppe* will align with him on his left and the *Truppenführer* will be the last in the line on the far left of the formation.

Figure 10-14

The command *„Gruppe, In Linie Zu Einem Gliede, Angetreten!"* At the command, the *Gruppenführer* signals his men by raising his hand above his head and shouting *„Gruppen, Angetreten!"* At the same time, the *Gruppenführer* should be locating himself directly in front of and facing the *Zugführer* in the *„Stillgestanden"* position. The next man to the the *Gruppenführer* will be the *Maschinengewehrschutz.* His two assistants will fall in next, also dressing on the *Gruppenführer.* The remainder of the *Gruppe* will fall in, with the *Truppenführer* checking the *Gruppe* from the end position on the far left of the formation. It will be the *Truppenführeren* job, while in formation, to keep the correct alignment of the unit. The *Gruppe* will always fall in at *„Stillgestanden"* and weapons will be at *„Gewehr, Ab."* When the *Gruppenführer* is in the position the *Zugführer* has designated as the forming point of the formation, the *Zugführer* is free to either move to his assigned position in formation or to stand directly in front of the formation and address the men.

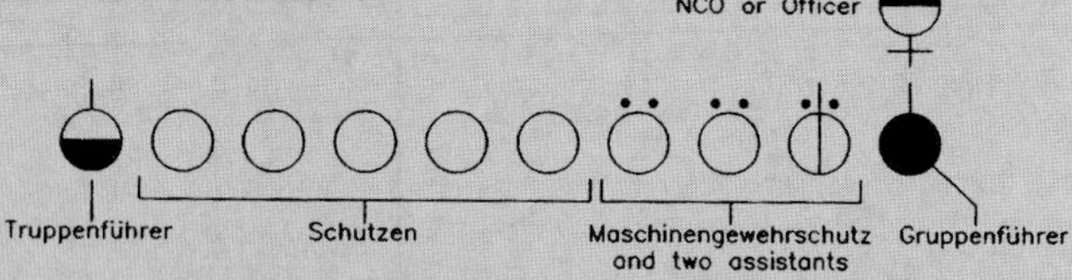

Figure 10-15

Note: for *Gruppe* training purposes, the *Gruppenführer* will be in charge of instructing his own men. The *Truppenführer* will assume the *Gruppenführeren* position and lead the *Gruppe* during this training period.

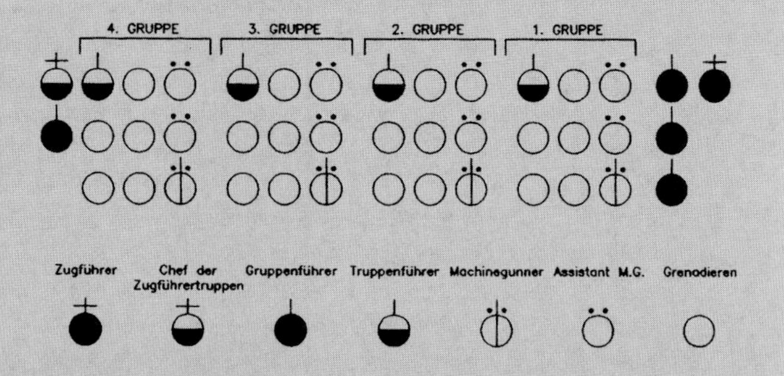

The formation for the *Zug* after 1942 is shown. It shows four *Gruppen* in formation and where the *Zugführer* and platoon sergeant stand.

B. *ZUG* or *Zug* is a platoon comprised of three or four *Gruppen*. The *Zugführer* (platoon leader) commands,a *Chef der Zugführertruppen* (platoon sergeant) is second in command, and each *Gruppe* has a *Gruppenführer* and *Truppenführer* as previously described in the *Gruppe* Training section. This model utilizes the 1942 *Zug* and *Kompanie* formation when sufficient numbers of troops are available to maintain this type. Below is an illustration of the 1942 Zug *„In Linie."* If there are not enough men to fill this type of formation, the *Zugführer* or *Kompanie Kommandeur* will order the early war type with the *Gruppen* aligned as previously shown *Gruppe* Training.

The command for *Zug* formation: *„Zug, In Linie, Angetreten!"* The command to *„Angetreten!"* can be given by either the *Zugführer* or the C*hef der Zugführertruppen*. Normally, the *Zugführer* will have the *Chef der Zugführertruppen* form the *Zug*. The person giving the command will assume the position where he wants the *1. Gruppe* to form up. When the command is given, the *1. Gruppenführer* will quickly move to his position directly in front of and facing the commander. As in *Gruppe* training, the *Gruppenführer* signals his men by raising his hand and calling out his *Gruppe*'s designated number, then moves to the *„Stillgestanden"* position. After *1. Gruppe* is formed, the *2. Gruppe* forms on the first and so on until all *Gruppen* are formed as in Figure 1. Note the placement of the other *Gruppenführeren* and the *Truppenführeren*. Illustrated above is the position of the *Zug* with everyone in place. This is also how the *Zug* would look in a *Kompanie* formation.

After the *Chef der Zugführertruppen* has formed the *Zug,* he will ask the *Gruppenführeren* for a head count and weapons tally. He then executes an "about face" and awaits the *Zugführer* to turn the command over to him. The *Chef der Zugführertruppen* salutes the *Zugführer* and reports, holding the salute until the total head and weapons count is given. Upon a return salute from the *Zugführer*, the *Chef der Zugführertruppen* executes an "about face" and returns to his position within the formation on the far left side. The *Zugführer* then addresses the *Zug* and gives the orders for the day. When he completes his address, he may call the *Chef der Zugführertruppen* to take command again by stating *„Zugführertruppen, Post."* The *Chef der Zugführertruppen* will move directly to the front of the *Zug* facing the *Zugführer*, salute, and take over the *Zug.* If the *Zug* has to move out directly, the *Zug führer* will normally command the movements.

Example of what the commanding officer or NCO will do during a Zug formation:

1. *„Angetreten!"* May use a whistle to alert the men and then the voice command to fall the men in.
2. *„Aufschliessen!, Angetreten!"* Inspect the ranks for alignment. All men should be elbow to elbow with no gaps in the ranks. Check for proper headgear, weapons, equipment, and uniforms.
3. *„Zug, Ruhrt Euch!"* If there will be a few minutes before the *Zugführer* or *Kompaniefuhrer* addresses the men, place the troops at ease. As the *Zugführer* or *Kompanieführer* nears the formation shout . . .
4. *„Stillgestanden!"* Officer or NCO in charge of the *Zug* should be standing centered, his

back to the *Zug,* and five paces to the front of the formation to receive the superior. Hand salute the superior.

5. *„Zug, Ruhrt Euch!“* If the superior officer or NCO is to address the troops or more than a few minutes, place the men at ease.
6. *„Stillgestanden!“* When the superior officer or NCO is finished, he will command the troops to attention.
7. *„Zugführertruppen, Post!“* The Chef der *Zugführertruppen* will move to the front of the formation, directly in front of the superior, hand salute, and take command of the *Zug* to dismiss the troops.
8. *„Zug, Wegtreten!“* If no other announcements are to be made, the *Zugführertruppen* will dismiss the men.

6. SALUTING IN THE WEHRMACHT

Every officer is the superior of all lower ranking officers and enlisted men; every noncommissioned officer is the superior of all privates; every noncommissioned officer in one of the first three grades is the superior of the lower ranking, noncommissioned officers in his own unit. There is no general rank superiority otherwise among noncommissioned officers or among the various grades of privates; however, all members of the armed services are obligated to “greet one another as a matter of military etiquette.”

7. GREETINGS IN THE WEHRMACHT

The German Army always addressed their officers and noncommissioned officers as *Herr* (Mr.) followed by their rank. However, in the *Waffen–ᛋᛋ,* the direct form of address is used, only by rank and last name, i.e., *Unterscharführer* Wessel or *Untersturmführer* Dietrich.

8. WEAPONS POSTION WHILE IN FORMATION

When the order *„Angetreten!“* is given, the men should fall in with the weapons in the following position:

1. *Gewehren – Gewehr, Ab* (order arms).
2. *Maschinenpistole/Sturmgewehr – Gewehr, Umhangen* (sling arms, right shoulder).
3. *Maschinengewehr* – Weapons grounded with bipod on right side of gunner.
4. *Granatwerfer* – Mortar is placed directly in front of the last man in the mortar team.
5. *Panzerfaust* or *Schreck* – Grounded on the right side of gunner with the front end forward.
6. Ammunition Boxes – Grounded to the bearer's right side with the latched end forward and the end of the box even with the muzzle end of the machine gun.

If *„Das Gewehr, Uber!“* is commanded, only the following weapons are affected:

1. *Gewehren* – Left shoulder arms.
2. *Maschinengewehr* – Left shoulder arms with pistol grip resting on chest and left hand supporting butt stock as with the rifle.
3. All other weapons and boxes remain where they are positioned.

The command *„Achtung! Prasentiert, das Gewehr!“* will affect only one weapon:

1. *Gewehren* – All rifles will move to the "present arms" position.

„Gewehr, Umhangen!“ is given and will affect the following weapons:

1. *Gewehren* – Slung over right shoulder.
2. *Maschinengewehr* – Slung over right shoulder, barrel up, and bipod folded.
3. *Granatwerfer* – Carried on the right side of the soldier by the base plate.

4. *Panzerfaust* – Placed over the left shoulder with the warhead end up.
5. *Panzerschreck* – Held vertically over left shoulder with muzzle end up.

If *„Gewehr, Ab!"* is commanded; return weapons to the positions described in *„Angetreten!"*

9. FORMING THE KOMPANIE

This is an example of what a wartime *Waffen-ᛋᛋ Kompanie* consisted of in the field. In reenacting today, there is no heavy weapons *Zug*, FLAK, or motorized APCs used in the field, yet. However, the LAH has two infantry *Kompanies* of three *Zugs* and is illustrated in. The figure represents the LᛋᛋAH in a 1942 and after formation *„Die Kompanie in Linie."*

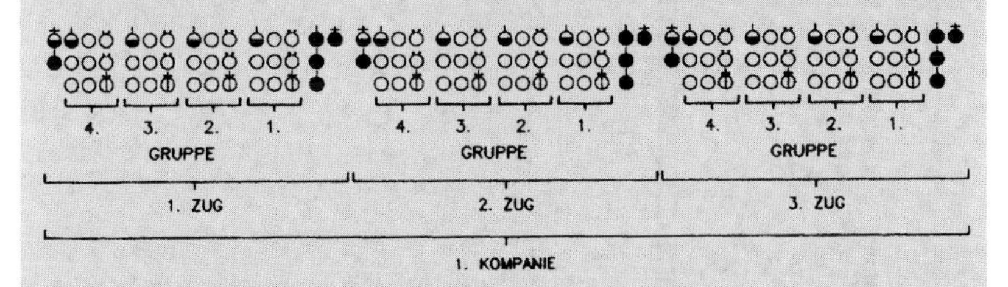

Figure 10-17

The command for *Kompanie* formation is *„Kompanie, In Linie, Angetreten!"* The *Kompanieführer* orders the *Kompanie* to form and should indicate to his *Zugführer* which direction he intends them to stand before issuing the *„Angetreten!"* command. On the order, the *Zugführer* will call their individual *Zug* to fall in. Care must be taken by the *Zugführer* to make sure his *Zug* is in proper position within the *Kompanie* formation. *1. Zug* is always on the far right of the formation, *2. Zug* is the middle unit, and the *3. Zug* is on the far left of the formation. Each *Zugführer* will stand directly in front of the position they want their *Zug* to form. It will be up to the *Gruppenführeren* to quickly position the *Gruppe* and to align on the *Zug* to his right. The *1. Gruppenführer* in *2.* and *3. Zug* must leave a space between himself and the C*hef der Zugführertruppen* of the adjacent unit, so his *Zugführer* is able to fall in with the *Zug*. At the time the *Zugführer* are falling in, the troops, they will face the formation. After the men are dressed and aligned, the *Zugführer „Kehrt Um!"* and face the *Kompanieführer*. When the *Kompanieführer* sees that the *Kompanie* is formed, he will command the Zugführers to "Post!" and they will *„Kehrt Um!"* once again and move to their places in the formation. The *Kompanieführer* will address the *Kompanie*. After the *Kompanieführer* has finished, he will order the Zugführers to "Post!" and they will move directly in front of their respective *Züge*. The *Kompanieführer* will order the *Zugführer* to carry out the day's mission at which time the Zugführers will hand salute *„Kehrt Um!"* and execute the day's orders to their *Züge*. If the *Kompanieführer* wants to meet with the *Zugführer* during his address, he may call the *Zugführer* from the formation for a conference. When this happens, the *Zugführer* should call the *Chef der Zugführertruppen* to stand before the *Zug* while the *Zugführer* is gone. The Zugführertruppen will stand directly in front of the Zug facing forward. When the Zugführers return, the Chef der *Zugführertruppen* automatically move to their respective positions in the formation without being told.

If the *Kompanieführer* wishes to inspect the *Kompanie*, he, the executive officer, and the *Spiess* (first sergeant) will move to the far right of the formation and inspect the *1. Zug*, moving down the line toward the *2. Zug*, etc. The *Kompanieführer* directs the *Spiess* to prepare the *Kompanie* for inspection. The *Spiess* hand salutes the *Kompanieführer*, executes a *„Kehrt Um!,"* and commands *„Ganze Kompanie, Stillgestanden!"* He will then *„Kehrt Um"* to face the *Kompanieführer* again, salutes, and states the *Kompanie* is ready for inspection. As the *Kompanieführer* and party arrive at the starting point of their

inspection *(1. Zug),* the *Spiess* orders, *„Kompanie, Augen, Recht!“* At the command, the entire unit looks right to follow the movement of the inspection team until they are directly in front of the men. At that time, the individual soldiers stop their head movement. The *Kompanieführer* and inspection team move back to the front of the *Kompanie* to address the men. If this is the last formation of the day (or just an inspection), the *Spiess* will be given the command by the Kompanieführer and dismiss the *Kompanie. Zugführer* will remain in the *Züge.* The *Spiess* will command, *„Nach Recht, Recht Euch!“* and after the *Kompanie* dresses right, he will order, *„ Wegtreten!“*
If the *Kompanie* is to be inspected while bearing arms, the *Spiess* will command just before eyes right, *„Kompanie, Das Gewehr, Uber!“* and then *„Achtung, Prasentiert, das Gewehr!“* The entire *Kompanie* will present arms as the inspection team begins its job. After the *Kompanie* is at "present arms," the *Spiess* will command *„Augen, Recht!“* When the inspection is complete, the *Spiess* will counter the orders by stating *„Kompanie, das Gewehr, Uber!“* The *Kompanie* cannot be dismissed from left shoulder arm position, so before the Spiess orders dismissal, he must command *„Das Gewehr, Ab!“* and then *„Kompanie, Wegtreten!“*

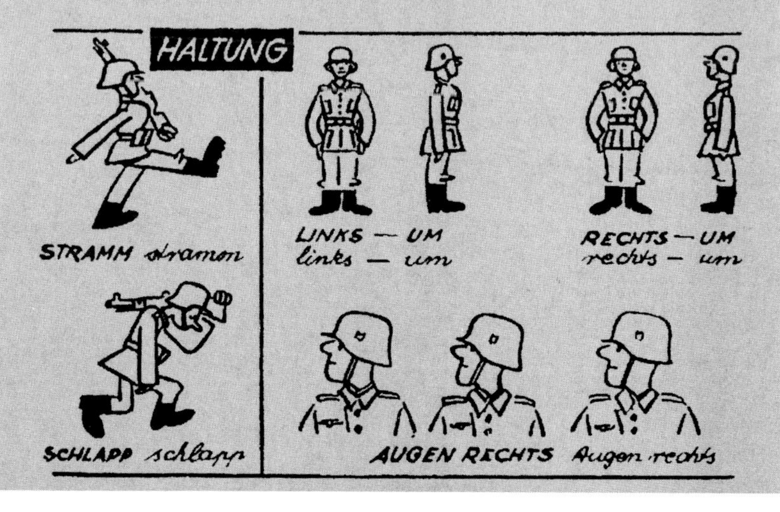

(The following is taken from 1. Btl. / ϟϟ–Pzgr. Rgtr. Lϟϟ-Pzgr. Rgt. LϟϟAH 2. Handbook, 2nd Edition, 1983.)

INTRODUCTION

Through WWII, tactics did evolve, and did change, and often observations made in 1940 were irrelevant by 1944. But the essence of change was still usually based on a coherent theory that merely changed in its application. The Germans concentrated in the theory on the small group and how to maximize its effectiveness.

First, the basic concepts behind the German training were very much different than the soon–to–be–enemy. In most of the pre–WWII training programs of the other nations, a actual problem would be presented by the training officer who should answer any questions about it and then dismiss the class for about an hour so the cadets might reflect upon the correct answer where they were recalled. In the German infantry classes, the same problem might be presented, BUT each of the students were expected to have a "workable" answer within two minutes. Maybe two or three of the fledglings would be called upon to present their solutions. The instructor would listen, then pick one cadet as *Gruppenführer* and have the class act out the proposed tactics immediately. Criticism was harsh and freely made both by the instructor and the cadet's peers. However, one element was seldom criticized. A student was NEVER chastised for the exhibition of "elan." Furthermore, quick decisions, even if they were wrong, were constantly encouraged.

Meanwhile, in the "Sandhurst" method, after the hour of pondering, the exercise would be discussed and maybe even acted out. But, unlike the Germans, the emphasis was completely different. There, recklessness was discouraged and a constant stress was made on the methodical conservation of resources as the objective is logically and correctly deduced. Following the evolution of the exercise, the instructor then would discuss it and further amplify the principles of method, conservation or coordination. And, since the Germans forced their exercises through with great immediacy and speed, while the rest pace it through, the German trainees would probably be able to study two or three tactical problems in the same time span it took the others to analyze but one.

Over in Russia, things were somewhat simplified, quite similar, in fact to WWII reenactments. Tactics were basically of two types: you either attacked or you defended. If you were defending, you simply stayed where your officer put you until the enemy was defeated, your officer ordered you elsewhere or you were dead. On the attack, you charged, closed with the enemy and killed him. Or you died trying. There was only one accepted excuse for failure, your death. Needless to say, this system does indeed explain to a large extent why the Russians had the highest casualty rate of any of the European participants.

In summation, we might say that in regards to initiative, the Germans encouraged it, the West forgot it and the Russians condemned it.

One of the more illustrative of the German methods was the "attack technique" in regards to an obstacle on the line of attack. This obstacle could be assume to be an enemy defense, possible dug–in and perhaps even with minefields and artillery support. But, despite the outward formidableness of the obstacle, a battalion was expected to be able to mount an attack, in complete coordination with the parent regiment, in no longer than thirty minutes from the time when the obstacle was first discovered. The principles for the battalion commander would be the same as those that would be used by his subordinates in the COMPANY and PLATOON level. The first step was to win the firefight *(Feuerkampf)* by quickly increasing the fire density on a particular section of the contact frontage. The point here was to establish a fire superiority on both a specific area and to a dictated depth. The actual evolution of this often followed a three–phase scenario.

The first phase was call *Niederhalten* or nailing down. In this phase, the foremost troops would stop movement and begin laying down an intensive fire in an attempt to stop all movements of the enemy. If artillery support was available, it would be used now. The intent was to make the enemy seek cover in his entrenchments, so that the individual squad leaders could make unhindered their basic terrain reconnaissances.

The next phase was called *Blinden* in which newly brought up troops would join the first ones to increase the fire to the point where the enemy defenses would be blinded to the now initiated movement of small groups attempting to penetrate the enemy position.

The last phase would take place after successful infiltration had been made into the soft spots of the enemy defense. The was the *Niederkampfen* in which the enemy would be beaten down by flanking and rearward fire from infiltrated units in addition to the previous units which still maintained an intense fire from the front. At this point, it was hoped that the defenders, demoralized by fire from all directions, would begin to bread and cease to function as an organized body. If that happened, it was all downhill and position would quickly crumble.

Throughout this phasing, the Germans stressed a number of points they wished their commanders to always keep in mind. The attack would be confined to a narrow frontage. For a battalion, this would be under 1,000 yards and hopefully about 600 yards. The attacking commander MUST concentrate all his firepower on the objective and disregard the flanks. It was assumed that the regimental people would protect his flanks while his battalion did its job.

Ausbildungsborschrift für die Infanterie Heft 2a Die Schutzenkompanie - Vom 16.3.1941

1. During the history of WWII reenacting, there has been no earnest effort made by any reenactment group other than the LAH in studying and adapting the correct German tactics. All German units have accepted the incorrect use of current U.S. tactics, and with minor changes, this pattern has continued during the entire lifetime of WWII reenacting. However, one must point out that the relevant German information, although available, was not common place in most reference sections of your local library. Yet, with all the emphasis being placed upon the authentic appearance, there was no one who was able or willing to explore and delve a little deeper into the correct German military methodology. Indeed, a great amount of work is necessary, but no more than in putting together a correct uniform or restoring the *Kubel.*

2. Now, in these sections, the correct information is available for all LAH members to learn. And, most excitingly, it will not take more than a few evenings of study and memorization to incorporate this information into your impression.

3. The information contained here was obtained from the U.S. War Department Military Service Information Bulletin No. 15 *The German Rifle Company,* an unedited reprint of the entire 1939 manual. These pages have been included for the historian to compare with the following excerpts from the 1942 edition which we will be using at all future reenactment.

4. As you will note in the comparisons of the two manuals, the most significant change was the reduction in *Gruppe* (squad) size from 13 to 10 men. Additionally the *Kompanie* formation was noticeably changed from *Gruppe* in line to *Gruppe* in march–order while standing

formation. These changes will be adhered to in the LAH, causing little if any difficulty in the change over.

5. The following pages clearly describe 1942 changes that we will be using. Please note, that only the basics are contained herein, and no effort has been made to describe the overall German tactical doctrine. This doctrine will be presented at the ϟϟ–*Unterführerschule.*

6. The 1942 *Gruppe,* as reorganized during March 1941 consists of 10. The *Gruppenführer* is the squad leader while the *Truppführer* is his assistant and represents him in case of necessity. He is also responsible for liaison with the *Zugführer* and adjacent squads.

7. The formations in figures 1,2 and 3 are assumed at once upon the following respective orders. Note that these are *Gruppe* commands; *Zug* formations and commands follow.

8. Figure 1: Squad line (one rank)
Command: *"Gruppe—In Linie zu einem Gleide! Antreten!"*
Pronunciation Guide: "Group–a—In leen-yeh tsso eye–nem glee–deh! On–trey–ten!"

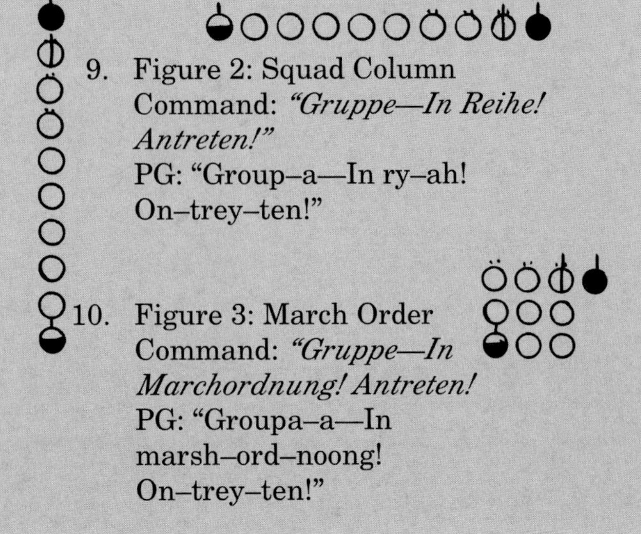

9. Figure 2: Squad Column
Command: *"Gruppe—In Reihe! Antreten!"*
PG: "Group–a—In ry–ah! On–trey–ten!"

10. Figure 3: March Order
Command: *"Gruppe—In Marchordnung! Antreten!*
PG: "Groupa–a—In marsh–ord–noong! On–trey–ten!"

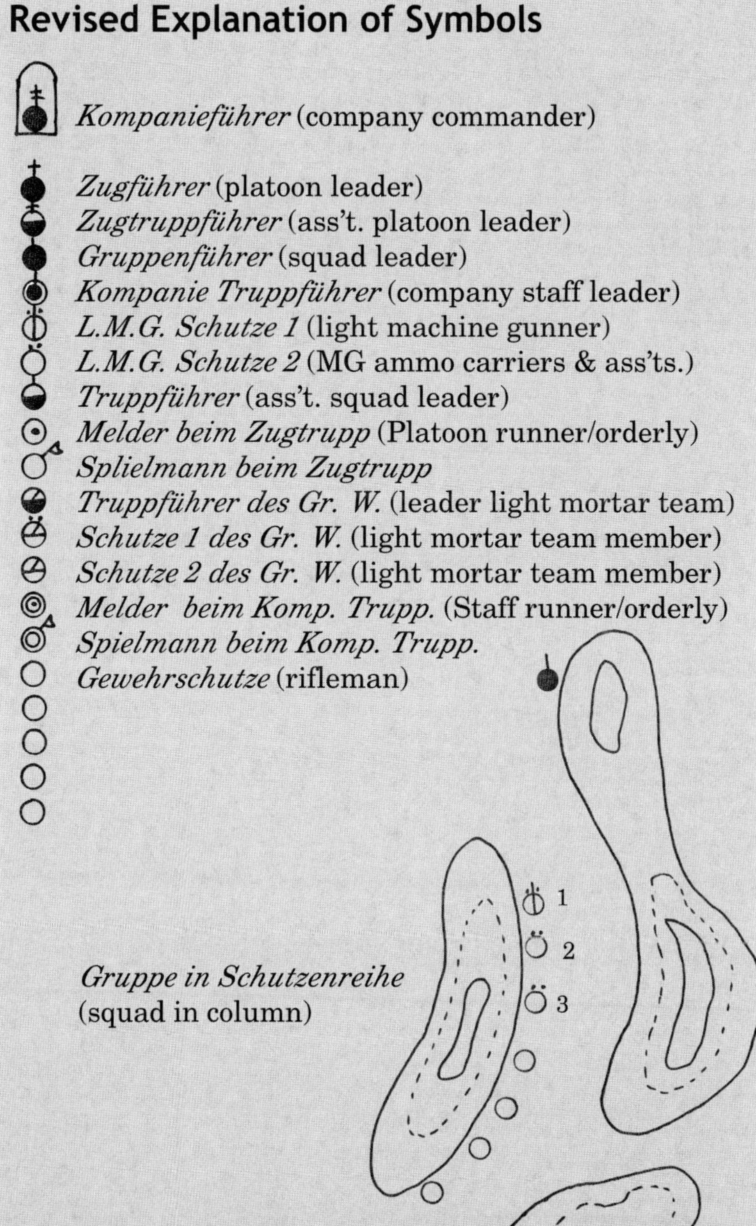
Revised Explanation of Symbols
Kompanieführer (company commander)
Zugführer (platoon leader)
Zugtruppführer (ass't. platoon leader)
Gruppenführer (squad leader)
Kompanie Truppführer (company staff leader)
L.M.G. Schutze 1 (light machine gunner)
L.M.G. Schutze 2 (MG ammo carriers & ass'ts.)
Truppführer (ass't. squad leader)
Melder beim Zugtrupp (Platoon runner/orderly)
Splielmann beim Zugtrupp
Truppführer des Gr. W. (leader light mortar team)
Schutze 1 des Gr. W. (light mortar team member)
Schutze 2 des Gr. W. (light mortar team member)
Melder beim Komp. Trupp. (Staff runner/orderly)
Spielmann beim Komp. Trupp.
Gewehrschutze (rifleman)
Gruppe in Schutzenreihe
(squad in column)
1
2
3

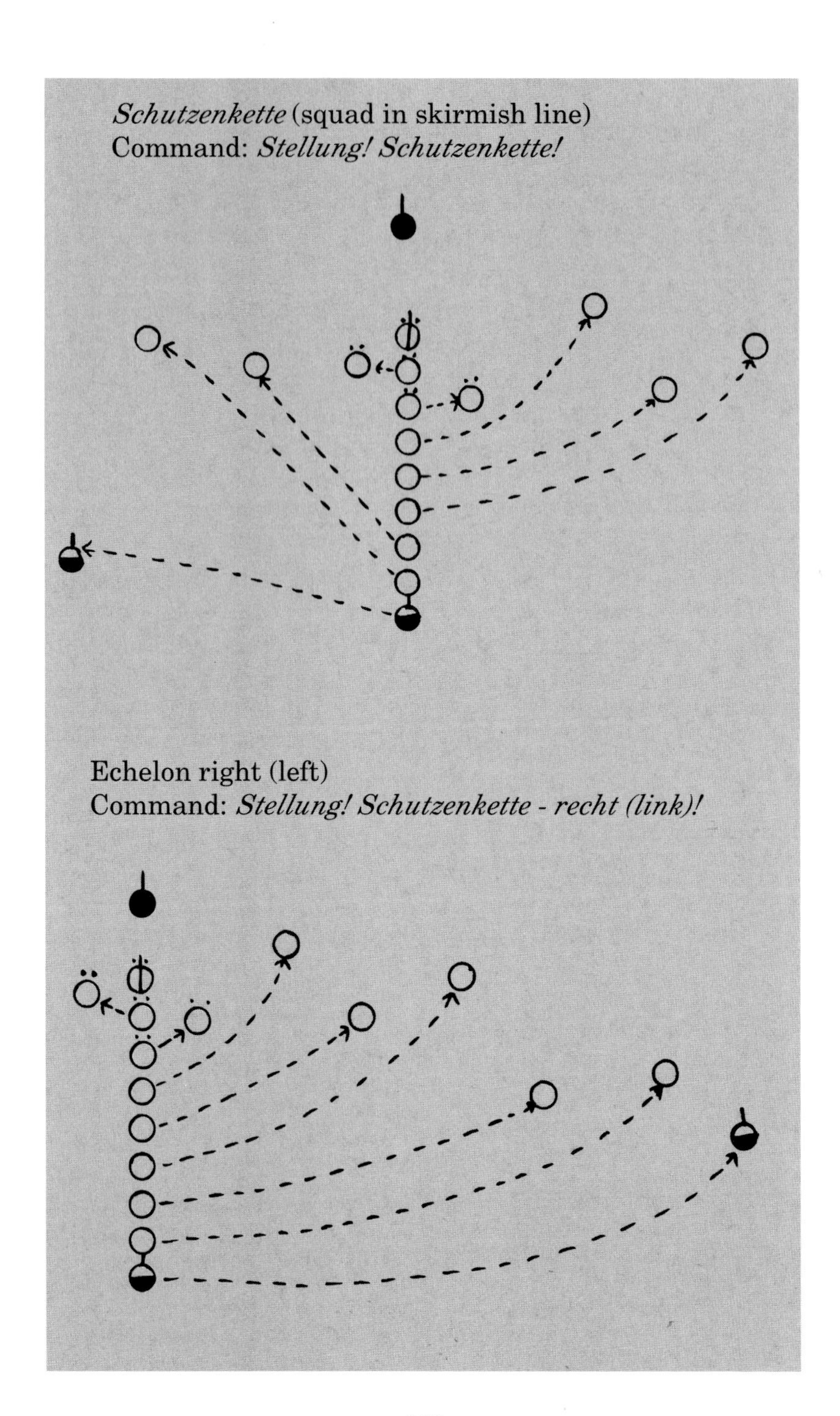
Schutzenkette (squad in skirmish line)
Command: *Stellung! Schutzenkette!*
Echelon right (left)
Command: *Stellung! Schutzenkette - recht (link)!*

11. As you have probably noticed, the major noticable change has occurred in the reduction of the number of men per *Gruppe.* You will note that the third rank is eliminated and the number 4 ammo carrier becomes another rifleman.

Der Schutzenzug

12. Figure 4: Platoon in Line
Command: *Zug - In Linie! Antreten!*

13. When comparing the 1942 platoon formation with that of 1939, the change in position of the *Gruppe* members is quite evident. Now, rather than having the *Gruppe* in line, they are positioned in a left–faced march–order with the *Gruppenführer* all remaining, except 4. *Gruppenführer,* on the extreme right. Although the reasoning for this major change is not clearly explained in the manual, the obvious supposition is that when in the marching order, it was easier to deploy into the typical combat formations.

14. Also note, that there are now four squads as opposed to the 1939 TOE of three *Gruppen,* although the total manpower available has not been noticable reduced. Actually, the firepower has been increased with the addition of one more machine gun.

15. The march order is identical except all the platoon members face to the front in the direction of the *Gruppenführer.* The *Zugführer* assumes his position on the extreme right and in line with squad leaders. (See Figure 4)

Platoon in Column
Command: *Entfaltung! Entlan diefer Mulde!*
Gruppen hintereinander!
Auseinanderziehen! Marsch! Marsch!

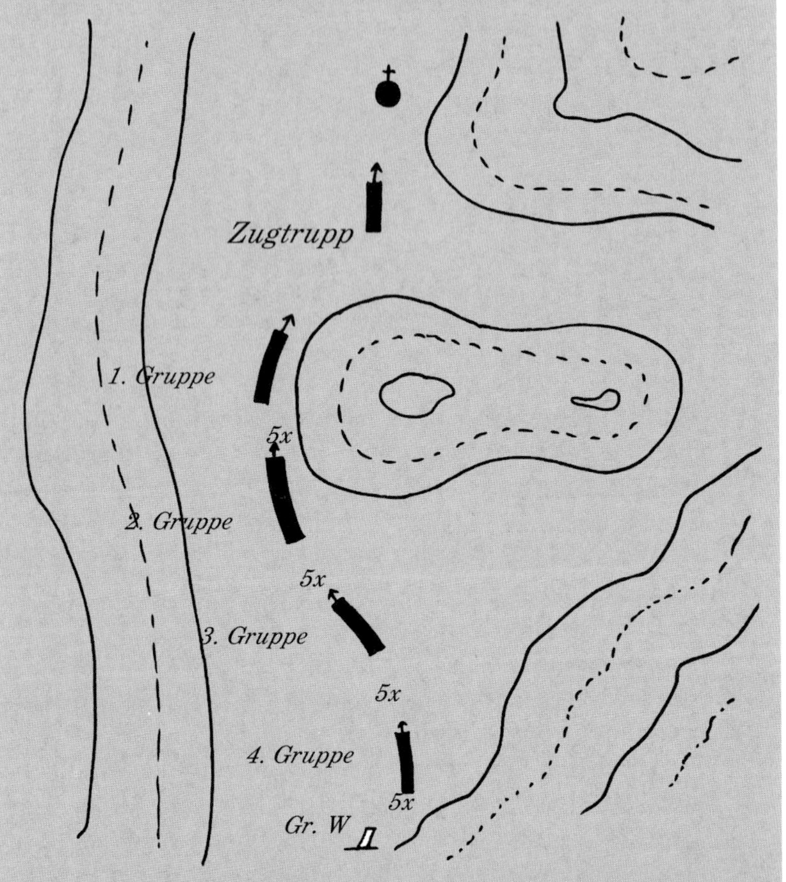

16. The organization of the March Column follows the standard doctrine of ll armies: the column is divided into the *Vorhut* (advance guard), *Gros* (main body) and *Nachhut* (rear guard). The advance and the rear guard are further subdivided. The advance guard into the *Spitze* (point), *Spitzenkompanie advance party), Vortrupp* (support troops) and *Haupttrupp* (reserve troops). Likewise,

the rear guard consists of the *Nachspitze* (rear point), *Nachspitzemkompanie* (rear party), *Nachtrupp* (support troops) and *Haupttrupp* (reserve troops).

The commander of the main unit/body usually marches at or near the head of the main body. Radio communication is maintained between this commander and both the advance and rear guards as well as with adjacent units marching along separate roads. In our reenactiments, normal movement is along roads, as was the usual travel of the German Army during the war. Whereas the contemporaries had to be greatly concerned about air attack, and therefore, ordered most movement at night, we do not have the same problem, allowing us freedom of movement during the daytime. Nevertheless, road movement is extremely hazardous and cross–country is must preferred, thereby lessening the chance of ambushes and enhancing our chance of envelopement of the enemy. As a rule, motorized units are assigned the protections of the flanks and rear of a march column; however, as a small unit/battalion, we may advance in a correct contemporary manner without these flank security detachments, simply by providing our own or doing without as both would be correct.

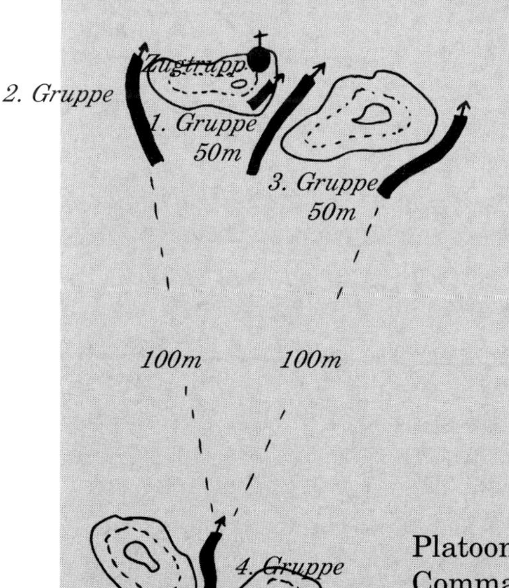

Platoon Wedge
Command: *Entfaltung! Richtung Kirchturm! 3 (2) Gruppen vorn! Auseinanderziehen! Marsch! Marsch!*

Employment of the Squad in Combat

Recapping, the *Panzergrenadierzug,* or rifle platoon, consists of the *Zugführer, Zugtruppführer (Chef der Zugführertruppen)* and *Stab* plus four *Gruppen* of ten men each and a three–man mortar team. (Figure 4)

The *Gruppe* is the smallest combat unit, consisting of the *Gruppenführer* and nine men, one of whom is the second–in–command, the *Truppführer.* (Figures. 2 & 3) Please note that these are positions of assignment rather than promotions, and they do not automatically carry promotions to higher grades with them. The *Truppführer* is the assistant of the squad leader and represents him in case of necessity. He is responsible for liaison with the *Zugführer* and adjacent *Gruppen.*

The *Gruppenführer* commands his squad, directs the fire of the light machine gun and, in so far as the combat permits, that of the riflemen also. He is responsible for the mechanical condition of the weapons and equipment, and for the availability of ammunition within his squad. In addition he is armed with field glasses, wire cutters, pocket compass, signal whistle, sunglasses and searchlight.

The machine gunner, No. 1, operates the MG in battle and is responsible for the care of the weapon. In addition to the MG and personal weapons, he is to have the tool pouch, short spade, sun glasses and spotlight.

The assistant, No. 2, is the assistant to the gunner in combat and insures the supply of ammunition. He assists the gunner in the preparation for firing and in going into position. Then he takes position under cover, several paces to the left flank or rear of the gunner, always ready to aid the gunner, for example, by helping to correct jams, changing barrels, righting the gun on bipod or replacing. After the gun has gone into position, if there is suitable cover present, he may lie down near the gunner to aid him in serving the gun and caring of the weapon. He is equipped with a barrel protector with a spare barrel, 200 round of ammunition, ammunition box with additional 300 rounds, short spade and sunglasses.

The ammunition carrier, No. 3, takes a position to the rear, under cover. He inspects the ammunition belts and ammunition and also operates as close–in or hand–to–hand fighter. He is equipped with a barrel–protector with a spare barrel, two ammunition boxes of 300 rounds each and a short spade.

The *Panzergrenadieren,* Nos. 4-9, including the *Trupp-führer,* execute the close–combat fighting with rifle fire and bayonet. They are equipped with rifle, ammunition pouches, short spade and, when ordered, hand grenades, smoke grenades, explosive charges, ammunition and MG tripod. When the situation, terrain, and hostile activity no longer permit close–order formation (Figure 4), the *Gruppe* deploys into open formation. The deployment of the *Gruppen* usually follows immediately after the platoon develops. It is executed upon signal, order or command.

Figure 4

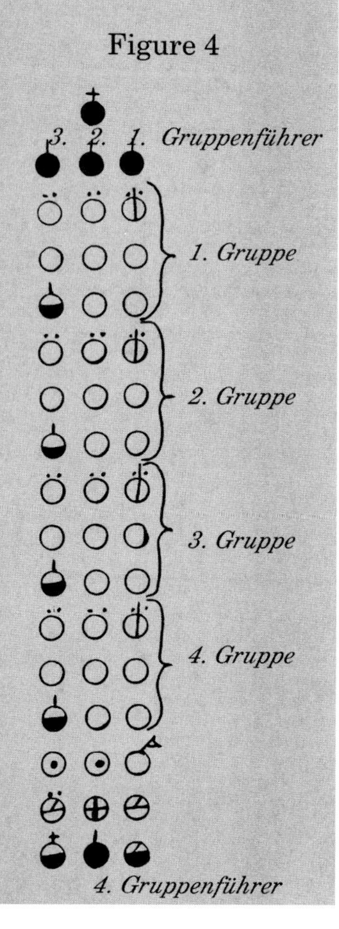

The principal deployed formations are the squad column (page 221) and the skirmish line (page 222). The *Gruppe* is always deployed as a unit, with the machine gunner, No. 1, as the base man.

The *Gruppe* in *Schutzen-reihe* Is used for approaching the enemy during the fire fight when only the light machine gun is firing and the riflemen are hald back. The *Truppführer* is at the tail of the column to insure that the members of the squad keep closed up.

If the immediate, combined fire action of both the machine gun and riflemen is required by the situation, the skirmish line formation should be adopted. If the whole squad is to engage simultaneously in the fire fight, the riflemen take positions according to the terrain, usually building up a skirmish on both sides of the machine gun, *Schutzenkette.* The machine gun remains, centrally located in the *Schutzenkette,* except where the terrain or situation requires the deployment of the riflemen to one side. *Stellung! Schutzenkette—Recht (Link).*

If it is desired to change the formation from *Schutzenreihe* to *Schutzenkette* in order to take up the fire fight immediately, the *Gruppenführer* gives the signal or command to deploy. Bunching around the machine gun must be avoided under all circumstances. When deploying, the base interval between men is approximately five paces, unless a different interval is expressly ordered. Remember to utilize all available cover when advancing, at the halt or withdrawing. This is more important than maintaining exact intervals.

If the deployment is executed from the march order, *Marschordnung,* the riflemen assume the same positions.

The use of other formations, or the omission of parts of squad, is permissible only when the situation makes it necessary. In this case special orders should be given. Cohesion of the *Gruppe* must be maintained at all times and at all costs.

The *Gruppe* formation may be changed from column to skirmish line, or vice–versa, to reduce casualties from hostile fire or to negotiate difficult terrain. Formation changes in rough terrain are often necessary in surmounting or avoiding obstacles of all kinds or in closing up on rear squads. It is less important that the distances and intervals be maintained exactly than it is that the *Gruppen* avoid losses—in other words, that it reach the enemy position in full strength. The attention of the riflemen should be directed more in the direction of the enemy and less on formation, remembering that this does not authorize the typical reenactment banzai charge.

The *Gruppenführer* is not restricted to any given position or place, however, as a RULE, he moves before his squad. This policy is predicated on the assumption that the *Gruppenführer* is the most experienced, knowledgable and thoroughly trained and is less apt to lead the *Gruppe* into ambush, etc. On occasion it may be necessary for him to leave his squad temporarily in order to observe the enemy, reconnoiter the terrain and maintain connection with the adjacent units. His place is then taken by the *Truppführer.*

In modern combat, the *Gruppe* is usually the largest unit which can be controlled by an individual leader on the battlefield. The squad is usually employed in combat at a UNIT. The fire fight is conducted the conducted as the concerted effort of the entire *Gruppe.*

If the situation requires the opening of fire—in the attack usually at the shorter ranges—the *Gruppenführer* as a rule, employs initially only the machine gun, the fire of which he personally directs. In many cases, for example if the target is small and the range short, it is preferable to employ a good rifle marksman.

In order to obtain the most effective results, the riflemen will be employed early. The employment should be effected at SHORT ranges and when the riflemen have sufficient cover so that they will not lied on the field of battle merely as targets. When the squad is organized for penetration, the riflemen are deployed in the front line in preparation for the final assault upon the defender. Those parts of the *Gruppe* which are not actually engaged in the fire fight are held under cover. However, the tactical integrity of the squad must be retained. The opening of fire is normally ordered by the *Gruppenführer.*

The employment of the light machine gun in the fire fight emphasizes the heaviest concentration of fire against the more threatening and most dangerous targets which may prevent the accomplishment of the combat mission. For effective distribution of fire, careful coordination with adjacent units and with the heavy infantry supporting weapon is essential.

When a *Gruppe* is operating under hostile fire, the breadth and depth of its deployed formation often render control of the entire *Gruppe* by one person very difficult. Therefore, the riflemen assist in the fire fight of the squad by conducting their fire independently, unless the *Gruppenführer* directs the concentration of the fire of his riflemen upon one target.

Light machine–gunners and riflemen cannot conduct a fire fight over a long period of time. An effort should always be made, therefore, so that they may go into position and fire without being discovered. Victory comes to the one who fires the largest number of well aimed shots against his opponent in the shortest time.

After a fire action of brief duration, or as soon as the purpose of the fire is attained, the light machine gunners take cover. In necessary, they move to another position. These changes in position must be made under cover, otherwise they will be worthless. Fire pauses should be utilized for improving the position.

If the terrain permits or the riflemen have dug in, the opening of fire is always prepared under cover. Not until then do the riflemen and the machine gunners go into position for fire by surprise. Every movement which is not used to good advantage weakens the fighting power of the *Gruppe.*

The conduct of a surprise fire attack is divided into preparation and execution. The initial preparation includes all activities which may be conducted under cover such a designation of targets, sight setting, distribution of extra ammunition, fire distribution, etc. The execution includes the occupation of positions and actual firing.

The employment of rifle fire must always be determined by the terrain and the situation. Using riflemen in surprise fire, the *Gruppenführer,* from a covered position, points out the targets to the riflemen before the beginning of fire and indicated the range and the target.

During the pauses in the firing, every rifleman and machine gunner must inspect independently his weapon and ammunition. The machine gun is always prepared to fire by have the bolt in the forward position and the ammunition belt in the firing position.

The essential thing in the fire fight is that the *Gruppenführer* recognizes the target quickly and correctly, points it out distinctly and briefly and gives the correct fire order. If several targets appear simultaneously, he must recognize and combat the one that is the most dangerous and most important at that time.

As an example, the *Gruppe* is entrenched as a combat group along a ridge. At about 1,500 yards, riflemen appear, advancing singly. The *Gruppe* should not open fire, either with the MG or the rifles, as the distance is such that there is little or no prospect of effective results. The *Gruppenführer* reports his observation to his *Zugführer* who in turn passes the information through the *Kompanieführer* to the *Battilonskommanduer.* The *Gruppenführer* retains the enemy under observation and prepares to open fire later.

In the next situation, three to four individuals are observed at 500 yards, carefully crawling forward, apparently a reconnaissance patrol. Nothing else is visible. Firing is withheld to permit the enemy to advance in order to take prisoners or to permit firing at a short, effective range.

Same situation, but close behind the enemy riflemen, a machine gun appears and is put into position 200 yards away. This is a paying target and also one which can make things very unpleasant for the squad. Open fire immediately with the light machine gun and rifles by quick designation of the target and brief fire order and strive for surprise attack. If you are unable to eliminate the enemy MG, cease fire and immediately move your MG to the alternative firing position.

Another situation may arise whereby you come under fire from a hostile MG. As *Gruppenführer,* you have located the MG but are unable to point it out to your gunner. Then you operate the MG in short bursts in order to designate the target to your gunner who, after siting the target, resumes control of the weapon.

The main thrusts of the hypothetical situations is to develop in the *Gruppenführer* the ability to adapt himself readily to various and unexpected situations, and on the basis of a sound decision made quickly, issue a brief and clear order.

The offensive implies a feeling of superiority. The attacker has initiative; he determines where and when the battle will be fought. Superiority in leadership, in the capacity of the troops (better training), in surprise, and in quick, active seizure and exploitation of favorable opportunities may lead to complete success against a numerically superior enemy.

The development, or *Entwicklung,* is normally the initial phase in preparation for the attack. It is the extension of the force both along the front and in depth—in short, a breaking up into smaller groups. During this phase, rifle companies leave the march route and break up into the three platoons. When the rifle platoon develops, its for *Gruppen* separate (Figures 5 & 6), but each squad remains in a close formation.

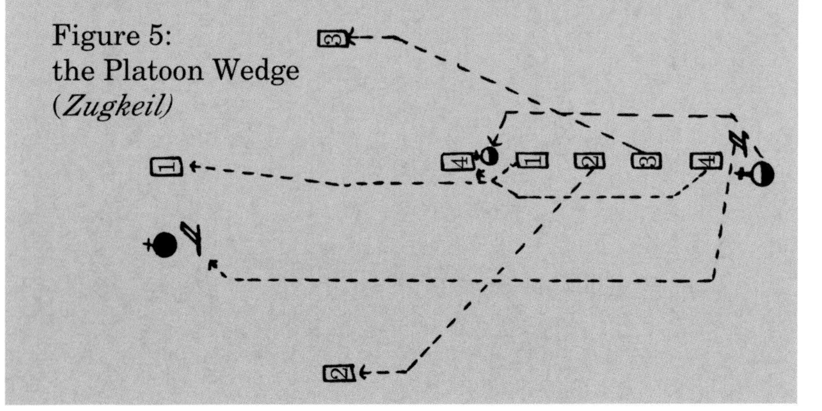

Figure 5:
the Platoon Wedge
(*Zugkeil*)

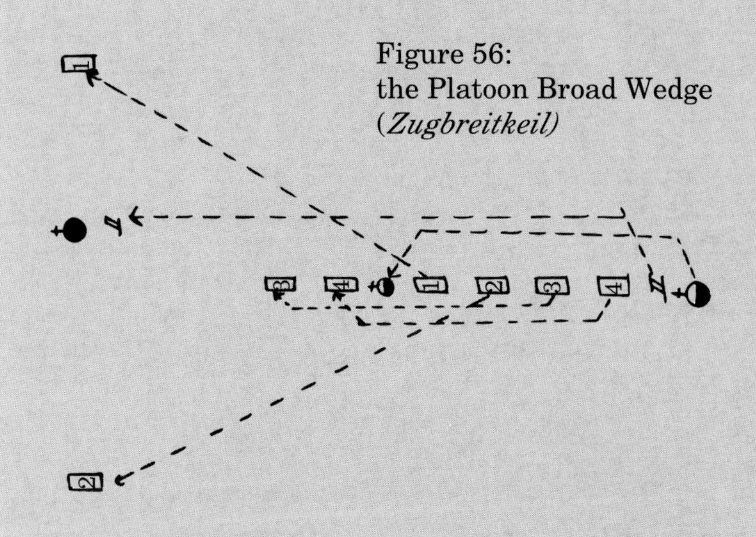

Figure 56:
the Platoon Broad Wedge
(*Zugbreitkeil*)

The *Zugführer* is not bound to any certain point. Other kinds of development are possible, and the distances and intervals are not fixed. Usually the order for development contained information of the enemy, objectives or purposes of the development and the formation.

The order may provide additional instructions such as special contact measures, direction of the advance, information pertaining to adjacent units, the advance of the heavy infantry weapons, the location of the platoon headquarters and of the light mortar section and the location of the *Zugführer*. For cxample,

> *Enemy still entrenched on the other side of the woods. The battalion reaches the woods in developed formation in order to attack the enemy. The company advances in developed formation to the right of the road. Platoon—PLATOON WEDGE, West, right corner of the forest, SPREAD OUT!*

All additional orders that are necessary are given after the development.

Deployment is the organization of troops for combat by disposing them in battle formations. The time to deploy is determined by the proximity of the enemy, by the terrain and by the necessity of opening fire. The deployment of the *Gruppe* usually follows immediately after the development of the *Zug.*

The *Gruppenführer* receives his mission from the *Zugführer.* Often, however, he will have to act independently within the limits of the platoon's mission.

The manner in which the squad advances in deployed formation depends on the terrain, the proximity of the enemy and the enemy fire action. In rough terrain, the squad column is usually the best formation by which the squad advances, taking advantage of depressions and any available cover. The *Gruppe* advances at a walk when it is under cover and receives no fire. Under fire, the *Gruppe* rushes as a unit or by individuals, takes cover where terrain permits, or opens fire.

The *Gruppe* works forward in extended formation. The *Gruppenführer* control and his influence on the action of the riflemen must be assured.

The MG group usually forms the spearhead of the attack with the *Gruppe.* The longer the riflemen are able to follow the MG in squad column, the longer the rear most, supporting MGs fire safely past the advancing *Gruppen* through existing gaps.

In working forward the men advance as a group or singly, by bounds or by crawling. The nature of the advance and the length of the bounds will depend on our own fire support, the enemy fire action and the terrain.

If the situation and enemy fire permit, the *Gruppenführer* takes advantage of the support of adjacent units, through *Truppführer* liaison, in order to permit the entire *Gruppe* to rush forward simultaneously. This method of advance should always be used when possible.

If the MG or riflemen are engaged in the fire fight before an advance is made, a change to the alternate firing position is first ordered. If the terrain permits, the gunner and the riflemen immediately lock their guns, take full cover and make all preparations for the bound. In the case of the MG, the gunner puts a full magazine in the magazine container, without pulling back the bold handle. As soon as the gunner is ready for the bound, he reports "Ready," *Fertig!*

When the MG goes into action, the assistant No. 2 sees that ammunition is available and supplements his supply from the ammunition carrier No .3. The latter sees that neither equipment nor ammunition is left in the last position. All the riflemen make themselves ready for the rush.

At the command 1. *Ganze Gruppe, Stellungswechfel vorbereitent! Rächster Sprung Hohlweg!* (Literal translation: Prepare to change position, through the defile by bounds!) The important words to note are entire squad *(Ganze Gruppe),* by bounds *(Sprungweise)* to the road *(an die Strasse. Marsch,* or *Ganze Gruppe! Sprungweise an die Strasse! Marsch!* On the command *Ganze Gruppe,* the *Gruppe* would prepare for the move.

The bound is ended by the command *Volle Deckung* (full cover) or *Stellung* (Position).

If the *Gruppe* does not become engaged in a fire fight, the command *Stellunswechfel* (Change positions) is not necessary and is not given. If the movement of the *Gruppe* has been seen and/or draws fire, however, the command is given and members of the *Gruppe* move a few paces in either direction while under cover.

If a movement or another bound is to be executed, the location is given as before. Often times, the command for the bound is replaced by signal or the simple order *Folgen* (Follow).

If the infantrymen are to go forward singly, then the objective to be reached is definitely indicated such as *Einzeln bis zum Weg, vorarbeiten!* (Forge ahead singly as far as ____.) *An die* ____. (To the____.) In this case it is important that the men lock their weapons, close their ammunition pouches and work forward independently at irregular intervals of time and space to the objective.

If there is frequent change of position, the *Gruppenführer* may have one gunner with ammunition (generally No. 2) advance forward. He selects the new gun position, prepares it, and places ammunition within reach under cover of the gunner (No. 1). He will then often take over and fire the MG when it is brought up to the position by the machine gunner (No. 1).

Attack

In the attack the fire fight is conducted initially by the heavy weapons. At effective ranges the MG is also employed. The riflemen participate in the fire fight in the early phases only when good results may be expected, or when they have sufficient cover. But it is not the task of the riflemen to engage in fire fights of long duration in order to gain fire superiority. In the attack, in the final analysis, it is the vigorous shock power of the riflemen (with bayonet) which overcomes the enemy. Fine leadership on the part of the *Gruppenführer* consists in bringing his riflemen into contact with the enemy in as strong conditions as is possible. The faster the leader brings his squad forward within the mission of the *Zug,* without exposing it to unnecessary losses, the greater will be his success. The outcome of the attack will depend upon the will of each individual soldier to attack, and particularly upon the will of the *Gruppenführer* .

If the squad, under the fire support of artillery and of the heavy infantry weapons, and by a careful exploitation of the terrain, has worked itself within effective rifle range, then its mission is to wrest fire superiority from the enemy. This requires strict fire discipline, the prerequisite for a successful fire fight. Fire effect is the most important consideration, taking precedent over cover. A guiding principle is: work forward as far a possible without firing, that is, so long as the fire support of the heavy infantry arms permits. The squad does not engage in the fire fight until the terrain no longer offers sufficient cover, or until the support of the other arms no longer suffices. In the latter care, the *Gruppe* will first open fire with the light MG against the enemy positions which offer resistance to further advance.

As an example, the *Gruppe* is lying in a depression, under cover; the *Gruppenführer* points out the target to No. 1. "At about 100 yards, a rock pile and on its left edge, a machine gun." No. 1 confirms the target and is then ordered to fire.

Only special reasons (as, for example, the loss of the MG in a critical situation, or the appearance of particularly favorable targets) would justify the temporary employment of the riflemen for a fire fight at mid–ranges.

Penetration *(Der Einbruch)*

Penetration into the enemy position often originates with the *Gruppenführer*. He seizes every opportunity for penetration, even without any special order. Usually a signal for the heavy arms to lift their fire will be given. In penetration, the whole *Gruppe* rushes or fires as a unit. If possible, the *Zugführer* employs several squads advancing from various directions against the objective. In this way, the defensive fire of the enemy will be scattered. This form of attack is no longer carried by the *Gruppe,* but by the *Zug.*

When the enemy is entrenched in strong points, it will be advantageous to throw hand grenades just before the assault. The throwing of grenades will then be limited to designated throwers. The *Gruppenführer* must assure that there is proper coordination and full cooperation between the throwers and the other riflemen and the MG.

The period of disorganization and confusion after the assault requires both special caution and vigorous action on the part of the *Gruppenführer*. He must hold what he has won. The *Gruppe,* which has become disorganized during the assault, must be quickly brought under full control by the *Gruppenführer*. Enemy counterattacks much find the *Gruppe* freed for defense.

If the *Gruppenführer* is given orders for the time of penetration *(der Einbruch),* he brings his riflemen forward to launch the assault at the moment fixed for penetration *(Angriffszeit).* At the point of the assault *(Angriffsstelle), the Gruppe* penetrates the enemy's position before he has had time to recover and to offer further resistance. To do this, terrain is captured by moving alternately at double time and at a walk. The riflemen follow the method of advance as undertaken by the *Gruppenführer.*

Every *Gruppenführer* takes advantage of any opportunities to penetrate or bread through the enemy position, even in the absence of orders. By his personal example he carries his *Gruppe* forward in the assault and breakthrough.

Before and during assault the enemy must be subjected to the greatest volume of fire by all available means. The L.MG. takes part in the assault and the breakthrough, firing even while in movement.

After the assault, the *Gruppe* should be quickly reorganized and prepared for further coordinated offensive action. Bunching up should be promptly remedied. The *Gruppe* should as soon as possible resume the advance deeper into the enemy position.

If the *Zugführer* orders one *Gruppe* to support (by fire) the advance and assault of the other squads, the *Gruppe* so designated concentrates its fire upon the place of penetration, or fires at the enemy in flanking or rear positions which are covering the point penetrated. Under these circumstances the L.MG. and all the rifles are employed at close ranges the sub–machine gun is also used.

Occupying the Position *(Das Befetzung and Halten einer Stellung)*

In occupying a position the *Gruppe* should be organized in such a way that the *Gruppenführer* can control the entire *Gruppe.* The front of the *Gruppe* is 30-40 yards.

The riflemen are grouped about the L.MG. within calling distance of each other. Some of the riflemen should always be located in close proximity to the L.MG.

In summary,

1. If at all possible, the *Gruppe* works forward under cover without actually firing, taking advantage of areas where there is little fire and where there is strong fire support by the heavy weapons.

2. The *Gruppenführer* need not, in advancing, restrict himself rigidly to the sector assigned. He should turn aside temporarily if by so doing he can avoid or minimize losses by the use of cover from observation and fire. However, he should not permit his men to bunch up, and he should also avoid masking the fire of the heavy machine guns in the rear.

3. The entrenching tools should always be make readily available prior to the first advance on the battlefield.

4. The *Gruppenführer* is not restricted to any given position. His place is at decisive points in the action, and where there exists the most responsibility. Until the *Gruppe has* started the fire fight, he always moves out rapidly at the head of his men and reconnoiters personally in order to determine by what routes, formations and methods he can advance his squad with the greatest possible protection and cover. The squad leader seeks out elevated points from which he can observe the enemy and the terrain. He leaves his *Gruppe* under cover and directs them by calls and signals.

5. Usually the L.MG. forms the spearhead of attack by the *Gruppe,* so that if necessary it can immediately support the squad by fire—if, for example, the *Gruppe comes* under fire.

6. In covered terrain, if there is the possibility of a sudden appearance of the enemy, the *Gruppenführer* has the riflemen move out ahead of the L.MG., thus providing better protection of the MG against surprise.

7. Every forward movement within sight of the enemy should be covered from the rear or adjacent weapons;

otherwise there will be heavy casualties. If necessary, the MG and the riflemen within the *Gruppe* provide mutual fire support.

8. Whether the members of the *Gruppe* rush forward together or individually depends upon the distance to the enemy, the effect of enemy weapons and the terrain (the nearest cover.) At longer distances, the members of the squad may often make one long bound together. As the distance to the enemy becomes shorter, the bounds must usually be proportionately decreased. As a general rule, the bounds should be short enough so that the fire aired at the men rushing forward will arrive too late—in other words, so that they will be hit during the bound.

9. When covered advance is no longer possible, fir by the squad is usually opened first with the L. MG. Every burst of fire, particularly that of the L.MG., takes the form of a surprise attack. In order to effect this surprise, it is necessary that the MG be made ready under cover and be well camouflaged. This is done while the *Gruppenführer* is surveying the objective and determining the range. If the MG is unsuccessful in effecting surprise fire, it may at short ranges often be destroyed by fire before it had the opportunity to fire itself.

10. First, the target which most hinders accomplishment of the mission should be engaged. The *Gruppenführer* must exploit every opportunity to fire upon large, close and clearly defined targets. The individual rifleman, when do definite target has been indicated, usually fires directly at the target nearest or most dangerous to him—at the target the fire of which hinders the advance of the *Gruppe.*

11. All riflemen should exploit at once every opportunity to win ground: for example, when the enemy opposite is under heavy fire or relaxes his fire. For this purpose, the *Gruppenführer* must from time to time exercise particularly close control over his men.

12. Moving the L.MG. to one side on uncovered terrain and under accurate enemy fire is useless, because the gun would be neutralized while changing position. If

there is no cover in the vicinity to which it can be withdrawn temporarily, the gun must endure the enemy fire and defend itself as best it can.

13. For the penetration, the *Gruppenführer* must take his *Gruppe* very firmly in hand, because his example is of utmost importance at this critical moment to lead his men forward to a vigorous assault.

GERMAN TACTICAL DOCTRINE: AN OVERVIEW

Prepared by ᛋᛋ–*Untersturmführer* P. Hanger, *Lehrinfanterieoffizier u. Bataillonsadjutant.*

"ONLY THE OFFENSIVE CAN ACHIEVE SUCCESS ON FIELD, PARTICULARLY WHEN COMBINED WITH THE ELEMENT OF SURPRISE. This need for aggressiveness has been emphasized during the past century and is applicable to all military operations.

"Implementation of this aggressive philosophy can only be attained by a highly trained officer and noncommissioned officer corps and a thoroughly disciplined army. Our tactical doctrine stresses the responsibility and the initiative of subordinated. The belief of former years that the German Army was inflexible and lacking in initiative has been completely destroyed in this war in which aggressive and daring leadership has been responsible for many bold decisions."

The defensive should be employed only as a holding operation or to provide a more secure base for future operations. Our defensive operations are only the beginning of the resumption of the offensive, and great stress must by placed upon the necessity of immediate and violent counterattacks. This defensive doctrine, while still embodying the correct principles has, through necessity, been modified, and the principle of defense in depth has been redeveloped using experience gained especially on the Russian front.

Retrograde movements, although usually considered a separate tactical movement, do encompass both of the above defensive principles. A retrograde, or withdrawal, is only undertaken when it is necessary to develop the aforementioned base of future operations.

German Offensive Operations:

The purpose of this section (and of the *Unterführerschule)* is to provide an insight into the training doctrine of the World War Two German soldier, NCOs and officers, thereby allowing us to more closely duplicate the German approach in our reenacting of the squad, platoon, *Kompanie* and battalion levels. It is not to provide a detailed study of the Grand Tactics involving divisions and armies; yet, an understanding of these Grand Tactics will help us to more clearly understand the German approach to all tactical doctrine and decisions.

As indicated in the overview, we can divide our tactical doctrine into three area:

1. Offensive Operations
2. Defensive Operations
3. Retrograde Operations.

Offensive operations can be subdivided into reconnaissance and attack.

Reconnaissance

"Information is valueless unless it can be delivered to the commander in time for him to act on it. This means that reconnaissance elements must be speedier than the troops following them and must possess highly effective means of communication. These two basic requirement throw into sharp relief the difficulties that beset tactical and combat reconnaissance for speedy task forces.

Mechanized reconnaissance units may execute both strategic and tactical reconnaissance. In the case of strategic reconnaissance, they function as army troops or as independent units operating between armies and groups of armies. They perform tactical reconnaissance for armored forces and other highly mobile bodies of troops, such as motorized infantry.

Tactical reconnaissance for infantry takes place within a narrow zone of limited depth; moreover both flanks usually are joined by other forces. This type of reconnaissance may be conducted by horse or motor reconnaissance.

Reconnaissance calls for highly mobile, flexible and easily handled units that possess a wide radius of action and good means of communication. Reconnaissance forces must observe and report the maximum, without being observed themselves. Therefore, the smaller the reconnaissance element and the more readily it lends itself to concealment, the easier the accomplishment of the mission. It must possess enough fighting power to be capable of defeating any similar opponent. Certain reconnaissance missions call for additional fighting; in such cases, the reconnaissance elements must be suitably reinforced." (Heinz Guderian on Armored Forces.)

Normal reconnaissance is carried out by the division reconnaissance battalion. Reconnaissance patrols are likely to be mixed and may include cyclists, motorcyclists, cavalry, armored cars or infantry, depending on the type of division and availability of the above. A relatively large number of antitank weapons are allocated to reconnaissance forces; this is also true of advance guards, in which antitank weapons are placed well forward.

The importance of reconnaissance was again stressed by General Jugin von Armin:

> *For correct handling of troops it is indispensable to know about the enemy. If one does not, one runs blindly into enemy fire. Therefore—reconnaissance and again reconnaissance! It must be carried out by sectors, from ridge to ridge...in exactly the same way as the attack—to ensure that the supporting weapons follow up in time.*

Do not dissipate reconnaissance strength. Superiority of means is very important for successful reconnaissance; BUT superiority in mobility and clever employment tend to offset numerical inferiority. It will frequently be necessary to fight for information. Advanced hostile security and reconnaissance forces must be penetrated or thrown back to make contact possible with the hostile main force. In this connection, it is often advisable to occupy important points quickly with motorized forces, if available. When there is great inferiority to the enemy, fighting should be avoided and an endeavor should be made to penetrate the enemy screen or go around it.

The commander who specifies what information is to be obtained should coordinate all his subordinate reconnaissance means. Efficient reconnaissance is not obtained through employment of large numbers of reconnoitering units, but by careful direction and instructions of these units as to what the commander wished to know. Definite missions and their relative urgency must be indicated, and the means of sending information to the rear, including definitely regulated traffic, must be insured.

While reconnaissance units must be prepared to fight to obtain the desired information, they will often be assigned supplementary tasks such as sabotage behind enemy lines and harassment of counter–reconnaissance.

Once again, only enough reconnaissance troops are sent on a mission to assure superiority in the area to be reconnoitered, remembering the superiority in mobility and clever employment will tend to offset numerical inferiority. Reserves must be kept close on hand to be committed when the reconnaissance must be intensified, when the original force meets strong enemy opposition and is unable to penetrate or flank the enemy, or when the direction and area to be reconnoitered are changed. If superior enemy forces are met, the reconnaissance patrol may fight a delaying action while other units, your reserve, flank the enemy.

Reconnaissance is classified as:

1. *Operative Aufklärung* (operational reconnaissance)
2. *Taktische Aufklärung* (tactical reconnaissance)
3. *Gefechtsaufklärung* (battle reconnaissance)

Operational reconnaissance, penetrating over a large area in great depth, provides the basis for strategic planning and action and is usually conducted by the *Luftwaffe* and motorized units. This type of reconnaissance will probably never be used in reenacting.

Tactical reconnaissance, carried out 15-20 miles in advance of the attacking force, provides the basis for the commitment of troops. Its mission embraces identification of the enemy's organization, disposition, strength and antiaircraft defense. It is concerned with his movements, bivouac areas, breadth and depth of his disposition, and especially important, the location of motorized and/or mechanized forces. For ground reconnaissance, the command utilized independent motorized reconnaissance battalions and reconnaissance battalions of the infantry.

Although this type of reconnaissance wills seldom be used during reenactments, both the orders and the results can be simulated by event coordinators.

In addition to the information needed on *Gefechtsbericht 301,* once the mission has been completed, or the reconnaissance element is directly in front of the supporting unit and in contact with the enemy, contact should be make with supporting unit, or appropriate commanding officer, to determine the element's next move, which would normally be to move all to a side and continue reconnaissance in that area, or to await relief from troops coming up in the rear, or to fall back upon the troops in the rear. In the absence of orders, the reconnaissance element would fall back upon the troops in the rear.

Battle reconnaissance, which will probably be utilized by our unit, as a rule is begun when the opposing begin to deploy. The purpose is to reconnoiter the enemy's front, flanks and rear to establish definitely the locations of his flanks, artillery, heavy infantry weapons and reserves.

Such reconnaissance locates our own front line and often provides close–in security and terrain reconnaissance.

In addition to normal reconnaissance elements, battle reconnaissance patrols may include infantry patrols, sometimes reinforced with light machine guns, heavy machine guns, light mortars, or antitank weapons' engineer patrols, which are particularly valuable in approaching a fortified area, a defile or a river; miscellaneous patrols including arterially patrols, etc.

The infantry patrols, the unit we are most concerned with, can be divided into:

1. *Spahtruppen* (battle reconnaissance patrol)
2. *Gefechtsspahtruppen (Stosstruppen)* (combat patrols)
3. *Spahtruppen mit besondren Aufgaben* (special patrols)
4. *Gelandeerkundung* (terrain reconnaissance)

The *Spahtruppen,* usually consisting of a half–section (4-5 men including and NCO) has the mission of obtaining such information as the location of enemy positions and minefields. They will generally avoid contact and retreat when fired upon.

The *Stosstruppen* consists of at least one NCO and eight men, nominally a complete *Gruppe,* but sometimes stronger, even consisting of two *Gruppen under* the command of a senior NCO or an officer. These are raiding parties, and their mission often includes bringing back POWs. Additionally they are often sent out to test the strength of enemy outposts. If an outpost proves to be weakly held, the patrol attacks, occupies the position and remains there until relieved by troops from the rear. If the post is strongly garrisoned, the patrol attempts to return with a POW.

Spahtruppen mit besonderen Aufgabe may vary in strength and are sent out to carry out such tasks as demolitions, engaging of enemy patrols that have penetrated our positions, and ambushing enemy columns.

Gelandderkundung are usually conducted by the *Pioniers*, and the mission is self–explanatory.

As noted, close–in reconnaissance is carried out by infantry patrols in addition to cavalry and cyclists parties and armored car patrols. The number and the strength of the patrols sent against the enemy, also their equipment and arms, depend on the situation and the mission. When available, the *Aufsklängs abgesonderte Truppenabtelung* will be utilized in the reconnaissance role, however regular infantry personnel may be utilized as necessary.

The reconnoitering patrol must move cautiously and quietly. They should halt frequently in order to observe and listen. Cunning and cleverness, a quick eye and resolute action, a love of adventure, and boldness are prerequisites for the successful execution of every reconnaissance mission. Your patrol should get as close to the enemy as possible without being seen in order that you may obtain information with the terrain so that on their return they may give information about it and if necessary, serve late as guides.

At night—often during the day, too—observation and listening posts are usually sent out in front to the line of sentinel posts to suitable points (for example, exits from villages, bridges, etc.) in order to provide increased security and information. The remain in position until relieved.

In crossing a sentry line, the visiting patrols must inform the nearest post of their mission and, when they return, of their observations. The same is true of reconnaissance patrols that are met.

Reconnaissance and visiting patrols within the line of outposts observe chiefly at night, and on broken terrain, intervening area not occupied by posts. The patrols also serve as liaison. As a rule, they consist of two men (including the leader) and are sent out by the out–guards.

Light motorized patrols, equipped with 4–wheeled armored cars or half–tracks, are employed on short–range tasks, liaison missions and observations. Patrols may be reinforced with engineers and motorcyclists to deal with road blocks and demolitions. Rifle companies belonging to the reconnaissance battalion may be attached to bread minor enemy resistance.

Each motorized patrol marches with a radio car in the rear. Commanding features are approached slowly, and following careful scrutiny, are rapidly passed. Parallel roads are covered successively. In scouting a wood, the leading car will drive towards the edge, halt briefly to observe, then drive off rapidly, hoping to draw fire which will disclose the enemy positions. At road blocks, the leading car will open fire. If fire is not returned, men will go forward to attach long tow roped to the road block. When necessary, men will dismount and proceed with sub-machine guns to reconnoiter on foot. Dismounted men are covered by the car guns. If obstacles prove formidable or are defended by antitank guns, patrols will report by radio. Pending orders, they will seek a detour. The commander may order the patrol to either bypass the obstacle to await reinforcement.

After receiving the information needed to formulate the type of offensive operations to be utilized, the commander will adhere to the German fundamental principle of offensive doctrine: ENCIRCLE AND DESTROY THE ENEMY! The objective of the combined arms, or task force, in attack is to bring the armored forces and the infantry into decisive action against the enemy with sufficient fire power and shock to accomplish the fundamental principle

the attack may be launched from one direction against the front, flank or rear; from several directions simultaneously; after penetration, into a new direction.

Realizing that even the most formidable forces are never sufficient for overwhelming superiority on the entire front, a point of main effort *(Schwerpunkt)* must be selected for a breakthrough while allotting narrow sectors of attack *(Gefechtsstreifen)* to the troops committed at the decisive locality. The other sectors of the front are engaged by weaker, diversionary forces.

In selecting the point of main effort, you must thoroughly work yourself into the situation by placing upon the situation map the location of your own troops and putting down the information that you have gained through reconnaissance about the enemy. This combat intelligence must be evaluated objectively; you must be extremely careful not to interpret what is received as you would like it to be or as you had hoped it would be.

Carefully read the orders received from the next higher commander (usually the host unit or scenario director) and consider all information received. In considering the situation, the follow principles govern:

1. The most important principle is to utilize to the maximum the available means. Any moderation in this regard is a deterring factor in attaining the ultimate goal.
2. Concentrate as much of your force as possible where you plan or believe the *Schwerpunkt* will fall, and expose yourself disadvantageously at other points in order to be more certain of success at the point of the main effort. The success of the main effort more than compensates for any minor losses sustained.
3. Lose no time! Unless special advantages accrue by delay, it is very important that you execute your plans as quickly as possible; through speedy action many measures of the enemy are nullified in their initial stages.
4. Weigh each situation independently, restricting yourself only to a consideration of the essentials. Ask yourself the following:
    - a) What is my mission?
    - b) Does it require decisive or delaying action?
    - c) Must I fight an independent action or will I be influenced by the movements or actions of other troops?
    - d) What is the condition of terrain between my troops and the enemy?
    - e) Where does the terrain permit approaches covered from air or land observation, for an attack on the enemy position?

f) When my mission requires defense, where does the terrain offer favorable defensive positions?

g) What possibilities are therefore available for the fulfillment of my mission?

h) What can the enemy do to counter my plan?

i) Where is the enemy now located?

J) Are there any bases for his strength and organization?

k) What can he do, making correct tactical suppositions?

l) Are there any indications that the enemy has acted incorrectly?

m) Do I know anything about the ability or personality of the commander or the conditions of his troops?

n) How will the terrain influence the enemy's actions?

o) How can I best fulfill my mission with the most damage to the enemy?

p) Where are my own troops?

q) Which are immediately available.

r) Which troops can later be drawn in? And when?

s) Are special transportation means such as trucks at my disposal?

t) What can I expect from my troops considering their past performance?

u) Is support from other organizations possible?

v) Which of the present possible solutions will give the greatest success?

w) As a result of all these considerations, is accomplishment of my mission no longer possible?

When, owing to unavoidable circumstances or unpredictable events, it is impossible to carry out a mission, then and only then may I change my mission, and I must select a substitute mission to assist effectively the general scheme of maneuver. I must notify at once the next highest commander in case I decide that it is impossible to carry out my assigned mission.

In general, when confronted by a vague situation and difficult circumstances, as is often the case in war, BE ACTIVE! Do not expect or await hints or suggestions from the enemy relative to your next move.

The decision must indicate a clear objective to be attained by the coordinated and aggressive use of available means. The strong will of the leader must dominate at all times; often the stronger will compels victory. Insure that all assistants clearly understand your plans.

Never hold a council of war. Complication and confusion are frequently introduced, and generally only an incomplete decision results. Do not hesitate to listen to the suggestions and proposals of Chief of Staff.

Part of the decision process will include the role or type of attack. Whether you are a *Kampfgruppeführer, Bataillonskammanduer* or a *Gruppenführer,* the only differences in the forms of attack is the number of personnel involved.

The frontal attack *(Frontalangriff)* is the difficult attack to execute successfully. Repeating: THE FRONTAL ATTACK IS THE MOST DIFFICULT ATTACK TO EXECUTE SUCCESSFULLY! It requires superiority in strength and produces decisive results only when the hostile front is penetrated. The frontage of the attack should be wider than the *Schwerpunkt,* in order to tie down the enemy on the flanks of the breakthrough. (The frontal attack is the most popular among reenactors and yet, it is the least authentic. The next time you observe a frontal assault by another unit or are contemplating one yourself, take a moment to reconsider this paragraph.)

The envelopment (*Unfassungsangriff*) is the most effective form of maneuver, and if aggressively employed deep in the hostile flank or rear, it can result in a most decisive victory or even annihilation of the enemy. An envelopment of both flanks presumes annihilation of the enemy. Wide envelopments are more effective than close–in. Among factors that contribute to successful envelopment are deception, concentration of strength at a critical point, available reserves, mobility and simplicity ofmaneuver. As to surprise, the enemy must not be given the time necessary to take countermeasures. As to mass, strength must be concentrated on the flank of the envelopment so that hostile extension of the line can be overrun or circumvented, and hostile defensive moves quickly and effectively frustrated. Do not let the envelopers become enveloped! As to fixing the enemy, the hostile forces in the front must be contained simultaneously with the enveloping attack.

While the *Unfassungsangrriff* is a combination of the frontal attack and a flank attack, the flank attack *(Flankenangriff)* is the most effective attack against the enemy's flank. This attack develops from the approach march, sometimes through a turning movement or from flank marches. In order to succeed, complete surprise must be achieved, and no time for countermeasures must be permitted. Since mobility and the deception of the enemy at other position re required, the flank attack is most successfully mounted from a distance.

An encirclement *(Einkreisung)* is a particularly decisive form of attack, but usually more difficult to execute than a flank attack or an envelopment. In an encirclement the enemy is not attacked all in the front, or is attack in front only by light forces, while the main attacking force passes entirely around him, with the objective maneuvering him out of position. The *Einkreisung* requires extreme mobility and deception.

After the decision to attack, and the mode thereof, has been made, the formal attack order *(Angriffsbefehl)* is issued, containing the following information:

1. Estimate of the situations including the disposition of friendly and hostile forces.
2. Mission
3. Assembly areas for the forward companies; objectives; sector boundaries; orders for the continuation of combat reconnaissance
4. Instructions for the preparation of the heavy–

weapons fire support

5. Assembly areas for the reserves
6. Time of the attack
7. Instructions for rear services (medical and supply)
8. Location of command posts
9. Miscellaneous

The width of a sector assigned to an infantry unit in the attack depends on the unit's mission and battle strength, on terrain conditions and on the probable strength of enemy resistance. Normally the sector assigned to a platoon is between 165-220 yards. A company attack sector is about 330-550 yards, while a battalion's is 440-1100 yards. The sectors are determined from the terrain reconnaissance although a map may be used. The important points always lie within a unit's sector unless they are to be attacked by several units. It is not necessary to occupy the whole width of the sector with troops, and open flanks ordinarily are not bounded. Note that road are NEVER used a sector boundaries but are rather included in a sector.

During the attack, the first stage is the *Entfaltung,* or shaking out. In this stage the battalion deploys down through company level. This shaking out can be generally accomplished during the assignment of tasks at most re-enactments The battalion proceeds under normal marching order with each segment (i.e. infantry, pioniers, reconnaissance, etc.) marching in *Kompanie* formations. The reconnaissance element is placed forward with the main strength of the battalion being kept under control of the *Bataillonskommanduer* as long as possible so that he may employ it in the most advantageous direction for the attack. If the condition of the terrain and enemy fire cause a change of intervals between elements, the normal elements are resumed as soon as possible.

Support weapons are used to cover the shaking out phase of deployment and subsequent advance, the weapons being kept within the march column between the companies/elements of the battalion.

After the first stage of deployment has been carried out, the *Bataillonskommanduer* marches with the leading elements and normally will send reconnaissance patrols ahead to reconnoiter the enemy. They may also be directed to seize important tactical features.

The second stage *(Entwicklung)* development, is deployment in detail, which is the final action of the company extending itself down to platoons and squads. The continued advance in columns (file) is considered desirable because it affords a small target and the battalion is easier to control; before adopting this formation, the danger of *enfilade* fire must be weighed. When the elements of the battalion are deployed, they exploit all possible cover as they advance, employing column–of–file formation with irregular intervals. The leading elements are not extended until they are to engage in a fire fight. The elements that follow continue to advance in file.

The attack on prepared positions is made a sequence of penetration, breakthrough and exploitation by reserves. The first phase is a series of local attacks by assault detachments with the aim of overcoming key points in the enemy defense, so that wedges into the enemy's forward positions can be established from which the attack can be driven forward into the depth of the enemy positions or rolling up the positions on either flank of the wedge.

Once a wedge has been firmly established in the enemy positions, the second phase of the attack begins. Troops so far held in their assembly area or slowly making forward progress under cover advance to cut the enemy position in two and to roll up the positions flanking the wedge.

This entire attack process can be illustrated by describing the April 1982 event at Weldon Spring, Missouri. At the usual morning formation, the *Leibstandarte* received their orders to proceed to the airfield and prepare defensive positions. Under command ᛋᛋ*–Hstuf.* Poddig, the LAH departed the assembly area in the normal marching order with three men abreast with the reconnaissance element as the lead unit followed by the 3. *Zug*. After leaving the assembly area and nearing the objective, the order was given for *Entfaltung*. All elements of the LAH immediately moved into a single–file march column with irregular intervals. As the column approached the objective, the advance element was ordered forward to seize the most prominent feature, the control tower. All three elements of "shaking–out" or *Entfaltung* were utilized:

1. Movement from March—Order to March—Column
2. Placement of one element forward
3. Seizure of an important tactical feature.

The second stage immediately followed with the remainder of the LAH proceeding forward in March–Column to the airfield where they began deployment in detail under the direction of their *Zugführeren*. At this time the reconnaissance troops *(Spahtruppen)* were pulled back and formed the reserve.

Shortly the enemy began to attack the defensive position. The *Bataillonskommanduer*, well aware of the axiom that the defensive is only a base for further offensive operations, directed the initiation of *Unfassungsangriff* by the reserve troops. Once again adhering to the principle of wide envelopments, the reserve began a forced cross-country march of over two miles that placed them in the rear of the enemy. At precisely the right moment, both elements of the defending force launched a simultaneous attack that resulted in the complete elimination of the enemy with minimal casualties to LAH.

As you can readily ascertain from this brief description, the utilization of completely authentic German tactics not only upgrades our living history impressions, they can be successfully used in the field.

Der alte Hase

Deutsch für Anfänger
Level 1 German
By Erich Tobey and Marsh Wise

This is the minimum level of command of the language and should be understood by every German reenactor. The amount of German contained in this section should enable the member at least to make himself understood in many situations, especially if he uses a little imagination, like coming out with *„Himmelwasser“* for rain (literally “sky-water”—the true term is *„Regen“*), etc. Especially effective in this hobby, however, is the memorization of just a few pertinent phrases—not a great number, but just a few, which you could mimic with the perfection of a genuine German. At the right time, you jabber forth with a short stream of perfect Teutonic speech. To the casual observer, it looks like you are Siegfried himself, and only you will know that all you are doing is utilizing the same talents found in the common Minah bird. The only thing you have to worry about is the other members getting tired of hearing the same phrase a half–dozen times in one weekend, but—You're learning German! See one of the fluent German speakers for new phrases!

The Germans always capitalize the first letter of nouns.

In German, the second letter of a vowel combination is long: the German word spelled “ei” is phonetically pronounced like “eye,” hence: zwei, (two) but “dienst,” (service or assignment)

“Ch” (or “hk” in our phonetic representation) is pronounced like the last sound in the Scottish “Loch,” or the composer “Bach,” but not so hard. Not a hard “K” sound.

The German "r" is a liquid consonant. Some dialects will put an almost theatrical trill on the r sound.

"S" at the beginning of a word is pronounced like a "Z." Inside a word it comes out "ss."

The German "J" is pronounced like the English "Y."

The German "W" is pronounced like the English "V."

The final "e" in German is pronounced with a short quality, e.g.: kleine (klin-ah), Herman Hesse (Hess-ah), etc. So, a German drives a Porsche, not a "Porsch."

German	Phonetic	English
ja	ja	yah
nein	nine	no
wer	vare	who
was	vahss	what
wann	vahn	when
wo	voe	where
warum	vah-**room**	why
wie	vee	how
ich	eesh	I
Sie	zee	you
er	air	he (it)
sie	zee	she (it)
es	ess	it
sie	zee	they
wir	veer	we
null	nool	0
eins	eints	1
zwei	zvai	2
drei	dry	3
vier	fear	4
fünf	fewnf	5
sechs	zeks	6
sieben	**zee**-ben	7
acht	ahkt	8
neun	noin	9
zehn	tsain	10
elf	elf	11
zwölf	tsvolf	12

German	Phonetic	English
essen	**ess**-en	eat
sclafen	**shlah**-fen	sleep
bleiben	**bly**-ben	stay
gehen	**gay**-en	go
trinken	**trink**-en	drink
kommen	**koe**-men	come
brauchen	**brow**-hken	need
austreten	**owss**-tray-ten	urinate
fragen	**frah**-gen	ask
antworten	**ahnt**-vor-ten	answer
machen	**mah**-hken	make
haben	**hah**-ben	have
sehen	**zay**-en	sehen
sein, ist, sind	zine	"to be," is, are
werfen	**vair**-fen	throw
geben	**gay**-ben	give
sagen	**zah**-gen	say
krank	krahnk	sick
gut	goot	good
schlecht	schlehkt	bad
groß	gross	big
klein	kline	small
schnell	shnell	fast
langsam	**lahng**-zahm	slow
neu	noi	new
alt	ahlt	old
Deutsch	doitsh	German
Englisch	**eng**-lish	English
Amerikanisch	ah-meir-i-**kahn**-ish	American
Russisch	**roo**-sish	Russian
feindliche	**fine**-leehk-eh	enemy
heiß	heiss	hot
kalt	kahlt	cold
Farbe	**far**-beh	color
grün	groon	green
blau	blau	blue
rot	rote	red
gelb	gelp	yellow

German	Phonetic	English
weiß	vice	white
braun	brown	brown
grau	grau	grey
schwarz	shvartz	black
hier	hear	here
da	dah	there
links	links	left
recht	rehkt	right
geradeaus	gey-rah-deh-**owss**	straight on
jetzt	yetst	now
später	**shpay**-ter	later
Heute	**hoi**-teh	today
Morgen	**mor**-gen	tomorrow
Gestern	**gess**-tern	yesterday
vor	for	before
nach	nahk	after
alles	**ah**-less	everything
mein	mine	my
Ihr	ear	your
sein	zine	his
und	oont	and
oder	**oh**-der	or
mit	mit	with
ohne	**oh**-ne	without
aber	**ah**-ber	but
für	fewyer	for
aus	owss	from
zu	tsoo	to
über	**ew**-ber	over
unter	**oon**-ter	under
hinter	**hin**-ter	behind
Baum	baum	tree
Weg	vek	path
Stein	stine	stone
Sonne	**zon**-eh	sun
Himmel	**him**-mell	ski
Höhe	**hoo**-eh	hill
Bach	bahk	creek

German	Phonetic	English
Mann	mahn	man
Frau	frau	woman
Kind	kint	child
Rauch	rauhk	smoke
Feuer	**foi**-er	fire
Tag	tahk	day
Nacht	nahkt	night
Wagen	**vah**-gen	vehicle
Flugzeug	**flook**-zoig	airplane
Gebaüde	geh-**boy**-deh	building
Tier	teer	animal
Boden	**bo**-den	ground
Wasser	**vah**-ser	water
Fuss	fooss	foot
Bein	bine	leg
Hand	handt	hand
Arm	ahrm	arm
Kopf	kawpf	head
Körper	**koor**-per	body
Stunde	**stoon**-deh	hour
Minute	mih-**noo**-teh	minute
Sekunde	zeh-**koon**-deh	second
Vogel	**foh**-gel	bird
Wanze	**vahn**-zeh	bug
Fisch	fish	fish
Pfanze	**flahn**-zeh	plant
Bekleidung	beh-**kly**-doong	clothing
Tasche	**tah**-sheh	pocket
Geld	gelt	money
Dolmetscher	**dole**-met-sher	interpeter
Gerausch	geh-**roish**	noise
zerstören	tser-**shtoor**-en	destroy
werden	**vair**-den	become
verloren	fair-**lor**-en	lose
finden	**fin**-den	find
laufen	**lau**-fen	run
setzen	**zet**-zen	sit
stehen	**shtey**-en	stand

German	Phonetic	English
Tür	tewr	door
Laub	laup	leaf
Fleisch	flaish	meat
Gemüse	geh-**mew**-zeh	vegetable
Wurst	voorst	sausage
Brot	brote	bread
Wieviel?	vee-**feel**	How Many?
Sind Sie sicher?	zint zee **zeehk-**er	Are you sure?
Wiefiel Uhr	vee-feel **oor**	what time
Ich bin...	eehk bin	I am...
Kommen Sie hier!	koh-men zee **heer**	Come here.
Ich verstehe nicht.	eehk fair-**shtay**-eh neehkt	I don't understand.
noch einmal	nohk **ein**-mahl	one more time
Wie sagt Mann auf Deutsch...	vee zahkt mahn auf **doytsh...**	How do you say in German...
Guten Tag.	goo-ten **tahk**	Hello.
Wie gehts?	vee **gayts**	How's it going?
Auf Wiedersehen.	auf **vee**-der-zay-en	Good bye.
Was ist das?	vahss isst **dahss**	What is that?
Bitte	bit-teh	Please
Danke	**dahnk**-eh	Thank you
Gern gesceneh	**gairn** geh-shay-en	You're welcome
Guten Abend.	goo-ten **ah**-bent	Good evening.
Verzeihung.	fair-**tsai**-oong	Excuse me.
Wie, bitte?	**vee,** bit-teh	What did you say?
Geben Sie mir...	**gay**-ben zee meer	Give me...
Das gefällt mir.	dahss geh-failt meer	I like that.
Das gefällt mir nicht.	dahss geh-failt meer **neehkt**	I don't like that.
Was halten Sie von...?	vahss **halt**-en zee fon	What is your opinion about...?
Nur auf Deutsch, bitte.	noor auf **doitsch,** bit-teh	Only in German, please.
Nicht wahr?	neehkt **var**	Isn't that so?
Unglaublich!	oon-**glaub**-leehk	Unbelieveable!
Es gibt...	ess **gipt**	There is (are)...

German	Phonetic	English
Was machen Sie?	vahss **mah**-hken zee	What are you doing?
Verstehen Sie?	fair-**shtay**-en zee	Do you understand?
Ruhe!	**roo**-eh	Quiet!
Beeilen Sie Sich!	bay-**eye**-len zee zish	Hurry up!
Es macht nichts!	es **mahkt** neehkts	It doesn't matter.
Paß auf!	pahss **auf**	Look out!
Mach schon!	mahk **shone**	OK, go on now.
Mensch!	mensh	Wow!
Natürlich!	nah-**tyewr**-lihk	Of course!
Machen Sie das nicht!	mah-hken zee ***dahss*** neehkt	Don't do that!
Mir nach!	meer **nahk**	Follow me!

German Military Terms and Phrases:

The purpose of the following section is to present a sampling of common German phrases for usage in the LϟϟAH and is not intended as a primer or course in the German language. The basic commands that may be encountered in any combat situation are usually included; however it is impossible to include the entire range of military commands. For further study in this area, the member is directed to the U.S. War Department TM 30-255, MILITARY DICTIONARY, published August 5, 1941 and subsequent editions. If this is not available in your local library, it can be obtained on interlibrary loan. Ask you local librarian for complete instructions.

(The following list compiled from information in the 1. Btl. / ϟϟ–Pzgr. Rgtr. Lϟϟ-Pzgr. Rgt. LϟϟAH 2. Handbook, 2nd Edition, 1983.)

German	English
Antreten! or *In Linie antreten!*	Fall in.
Stillgestanden!	Attentention.
Nach rechts (links)...richt euch!	Dress right (left)...dress.
Die Augen...recht (links)!	Eyes right (left).
Rechts um!	Right face.
Links um!	Left face.
Kehrt! or *Kehrt um!*	About face.
Rührt euch!	At ease.
Nach rechts...richt euch!	Dress right...dress.
Augen gerade...aus!	Ready...front.
Grundstellung!	Attention; as you were.
Achtung! Präsentiert das... Gewehr!	Present...arms.
Geweht ab!	Order...arms!
Das Gewehr...über!	Shoulder...arms!
Gewehr unhangen!	Sling arms!
Linie	Line
Reihe	Column (file)
Marschordnung	March order
In Marschordnun antreten!	In march-order...fall in.
Ohne Tritt...marsch!	Route step
(If this command is not given, all troops automatically march in step.)	
Im Marschordnung...antreten!	March...order.
Marsch!	Forward, march.
Marsch! Marsch!	Double time.
Rechts Schwenkt...marsch!	Column right...march.
Links Schwenkt...marsch!	Column left...march.
Rechts (links) ...um! (Marching)	By the right (left) flank... march.
Rechts (links) schwenkt...marsch!	Column right (left)... march.
Ganze Abteilung...kehrt!	Detail, about face.
Abteilung...marsch!	Detail, forward march.
Abteling (Kompanie,Zug, etc.)... halt!	Halt.
Fertig zum aufprotzen!	Prepare to limber.
Protzt auf (ab)!	(Un) limber.

German	English
An die Fahrzeuge!	Prepare to mount.
Fertig zu aufsitzen (absitzen)!	Prepare to (dis-)mount.
Abgesessen! or *Absitzen!*	Dismount.
Wegtreten!	Dismissed.
Hinter dem Geschütz antreten! (arty)	Posts
Stellung! Augen Richtung!	Action front
Zum Feuern nach rechts (links)!`	Action...right (left).
Nach rückwärts protzt ab! (Arty)	Action rear
Zum Feuern nach rechts (links)!	Action...right (left)
All Geschütztürme bemannt und feuerbereit!	All turrents manned and ready.
Achtung!	Attention (to orders).
An die Gewehre! or *An die Karabinert!*	Behind stacks...Fall in.
Zum Schiessen antreten!	Next on the firing line.
An die Gewehre! or *An die Karabiner!*	Prepare to take arms.
Gewehre in die...Hand!	Take...arms.
Laden und Sichern!	Load and lock.
Entlanden!	Unload.
Durchladen!	Finish loading.
Feuer kreuzen!	Concentrate fire.
Geradeaus!	Forward.
Fertig!	Ready.
Schuss! or *Feuer!*	Fire.
Kürzer!	Shorten range.
Feuer frei!	Fire at will.
Stellung! Feuer frei!	Into action. Fire at will.
Treffer! or *Schuss lieft im Zeil!* (Arty)	Hit
Stopfen! Halt! or *Feuerpause!*	Cease fire.
Zum Schiessen...antreten!	Next order on firing line.
Seitengewehr pflanzt...auf!	Fix...bayonets.
Seitengewehr an Ort!	Unfix bayonets.
Setzt die Gewehre...zusammen!	Stack...arms.
Gut, der Mann!	Attaboy!

German	English
Tagesbefehl	Order of the day
Licht aus! or *Feuer aus!*	Lights out.
Spähtrupps	Reconnaissance troops
Stosstruppen	Assault trops
Kradmelder	Dispatch rider
Thermokübel	Hot food container
ᛋᛋ Soldaten	ᛋᛋ soldiers
Panzerspahwagon	armored scout car
Beobachter	Observer
Schuss lag weit!	Over
Vorsicht!	Careful
Aufpassen!	Look out.
Knieen!	Kneel.
Hinlegen!	(Lie) down.
Nieder!	Down.
Aufstehen!	Stand up.
Auf!	Up.
Zeigen Sie mir Ihren Ausweis!	Identify yourself.
Warten Sie hier!	Wait here.
Vortreten!	Come forward.
Züruck!	Move back.
Rumdrehen!	Turn around.
Vorwärts!	Go ahead.
Folgen Sie mir (ihm).	Follow me (him).
Schnell! Rasch!	Quickly. Hurry.
Langsam gehen!	Go slowly.
Halt!	Stop.
Sofort!	Right away.
Rühe!	Quiet.
Halt! Wer da?	Halt. Who's there?
Ergeben Sie sich.	Surrender.
Waffen niederlegen!	Throw down your arms.
Hände hoch!	Raise your hands.
Keine Bewegung!	Dont't move.
Machen Sie keine Geschichten!	Don't try any tricks.
Nicht schiessen!	Don't shoot.
Antreten hier (dort).	Line up here there).
Guten Morgen (Nacht).	Good morning (night).

German	English
Guten Tag.	Good day or afternoon.
Wie geht es Ihnen?	How are you?
Es geht mir gut.	I am well.
Danke.	Thank you.
Bitte.	You're welcome. or Please.
Wie heissen Sie?	What is your name?
Ich heisse....	My name is....
Sehn angenehm.	Glad to meet you.
Wollen Sie eine Zigarette?	Will you have a cigarette?
Haben Sie...?	Do you have...?
Leben Sie wohl.	Good-bye.
Ja	Yes
Nein	No
Veilleicht	Maybe
Bestimmt	Certainly
Ich weiss nicht.	Idon't know.
Ich glaube nicht.	I don't think so.
Sprechen Sie...?	Do you speak...?
Ich spreche....	Ich speak....
Verstehen Sie?	Do you understand?
Ich vestehe (nicht).	I (don't) understand.
Wie bitte?	What?
Wie nennen Sie das?	What do you call this?
Was is dies (das)?	What is this (that)?
Kommen Sie mit mir!	Come with me.
Es wird Ihnen nichts geschehen.	You will not be hurt.
Zeigen Sie Ihren Ausweis!	Show your ID.
Welchen Rank haben Sie?	What is your rank?
Welches ist Ihre Einheit (Kompanie, Truppenteil)?	What is your outfit (company, branch of service)?
Seit wann sind Sie im Dienst?	How long have you been in the service?

Radio Communications	
German	**English**
_____, von _____.	_____, this is _____.
_____ Kommen.	Calling _____.
Kommen.	Over (Go ahead).
Warten	Wait
Irrung	Correction
Trennung	Break
Bitte prüfen.	Verify.
Bitte Quittung.	Acknowledge
Bitte, wiederholen.	Say again.
Lautstärke _____.	Readability _____.
eins	unreadable
zwei	poor
drei	fair
vier	good
fünf	perfectly readable
Ende	That is all.
K.R.	Urgent
Keine Quittung	Do not answer.

A	*nton*	*O*	*tto*
Ä	*rger*	*Ö*	*dipus*
B	*ertha*	*P*	*aula*
C	*asar*	*Q*	*uelle*
CH	*arlotte*	*R*	*ichard*
D	*ora*	*S*	*iegfried*
E	*mil*	*T*	*heodor*
F	*riedrich*	*U*	*lrich*
G	*ustav*	*Ü*	*bel*
H	*einrich*	*V*	*iktor*
I	*da*	*W*	*ilhelm*
J	*ulius*	*X*	*anthippe*
K	*onrad*	*Y*	*psilon*
L	*udwig*	*Z*	*eppelin*
M	*artha*	*SCH*	*ule*
N	*ordpot*		

KB Zug Lehmann

The majority of photos are by the *Soldat FHQ Kriegsberichter Zug Lehmann,* in particular:

Rachel Putnam

Robert Kelleher

Cyrus Lee

Additionally the following acted as *Sonderphotograph u. Kriegsberichter* for either *KB Zug Lehmann* or their units:

Kevin Poole – *KB Zug Lehmann*
John Figueroa – *KB Panzer Lehr*
Travis Jacobsen – *KB 12. ᛋᛋ "Hitlerjugend"*
Joseph Starost – *3. / ᛋᛋ Aufklarung Abt. 'Hitlerjugend"*
Randy Arneson – *KB. 1. ᛋᛋ LᛋᛋAH*
Mike Bollow – *KB. 2. Panzer u. 116 Panzer "Windhund"*
Mike Dunn – *KB. Feldgendarmerie Trupp 200*
Clauido Ortillie u. Fergus Mc Leod – *KB Zug Lehmann*
Tony Dudmann – *KB Zug Lehmann*
Erin Warfield – *KB Deutsche Rotes Kreuz Helferin*

Color *Fotos*

A beautifully done eastern Volunteer Impression created by this reenactor to include the cap saber device.

This was one of several *Kriegsmarine* uniform variation this reenactor has created. Next comes the vessel!

A study of the *Wintertarnanzug* with the white side exposed.

A study of both the *Heer* camoflage patterns. The gloves are not correct.

This SS–Mann wears the *Feldbluse 44* and is carrying a *Panzerfaust 60M.*

Men of *LSSAH* in *Tarnhemd.*

A study of the *Luftwaffe Fleigerbluse* and *Fallschirm-jägerhose* worn by the *Zug-führer* as he prepares a *Jäger* for a parade.

An after–the–battle *Foto* of a *FJ Zug.* An example to any group of reenactors, not only in appearance but performance!

A study of *FJ Knockensack* and equipment.

Munitionsbandolier and magazine pouch for the G or K43.

A study of HBT uniforms and bicycles.

Feldgrau is not all the same color!

A study of the tropical uniform.

One of many fantastic pieces of vehicle fabrication, *Dagmar* was built from plans based on scaled–up model kit pieces put onto a OT10 chassis!

Deutsche Rotes Kreuz Helferin or nurse impression.

Nachrichtenhelferine des Heeres or Army Signal Auxiliaries.